MAN, THE MANIPULATOR

MAN, THE MANIPULATOR

*The Inner Journey from Manipulation
to Actualization*

Everett L. Shostrom

ABINGDON PRESS
NASHVILLE & NEW YORK

MAN, THE MANIPULATOR

Copyright © 1967 by Abingdon Press

ISBN 0-687-23074-8

Library of Congress Catalog Card Number: 67-15947

The material on pp. 121-28 is adapted from
Lawrence M. Brammer and Everett L. Shostrom,
Therapeutic Psychology, © 1960. By permission of
Prentice-Hall, Inc., Englewood Cliffs, New Jersey.

SET UP, PRINTED, AND BOUND BY THE
PARTHENON PRESS, AT NASHVILLE,
TENNESSEE, UNITED STATES OF AMERICA

To My Mother and Father
Franz and Hilma Shostrom
Two Actualizing Senior Citizens

FOREWORD

A few years ago, I came across a paperback called *A Cow Can't Live in Los Angeles*. It told of a Mexican who smuggled his relatives into this country and said to them, "Look here, Americans are a very nice kind of people, but there is one point where they are very touchy. You must not let them know that they are corpses." I believe this exactly describes man's "sickness" today. Modern man is dead, a puppet. This corpse-like behavior is a part of every modern man. He is deliberate and without emotions

7

—a marionette. He is reliable, but without live intentions, wishes, wants, and desires. His life is very boring, empty, and meaningless. He controls and manipulates others and is caught in the web of his own manipulations.

The purpose of this book is to describe how we have petrified ourselves into manipulators playing roles—often phony roles—without any support from our heart, without any support from our wish to be and to live. It is very difficult for modern man to realize and to accept the fact that he is dead, that he is a phony, and that he is missing out on being alive and being fully human. Nevertheless, he can again feel his humanness once he is willing to risk, to open up, and to become alive, and thus he moves from the deadness and deliberateness of manipulation to the integrated spontaneity of actualization.

I believe that the continuum of deadness to aliveness (or from manipulation to actualization) described in this book should be substituted for the continuum of sickness to health so commonly used in psychiatric and psychological circles. Inherent in this continuum is the important notion of hope. To become aware of one's manipulations is a first step, but actually to believe that out of these manipulations can grow actualizing potentials—this is the hope. As Erik Erickson says, "We recognize . . . an inner affinity between the . . . deepest mental disturbances and a radical loss of a basic kind of hope." For years now, it has been clear that such hope has been missing in contemporary psychiatry and psychology, and a post-Freudian revolution is in progress.

There is, furthermore, a growing disillusionment with the "medical model" of people as being either sick or well. No longer can the patient of a great majority of therapists be termed a psychotic or even a classical neurotic. He is a *person* who has problems of living and has developed manipulative patterns of behavior which are self-defeating.

Equally important is the recognition that "mental illness" is an inappropriate term for describing such people. The writings of Thomas Szasz and others all point to the fact that the use of the medical model for troubled persons is inaccurate, for it implies that there is some altered bodily state rather than a maladaptive behavior problem. Further, it gives the patient an excuse for remaining troubled. Common are such comments from patients as, "I'm sick, I can't help it"; "Don't blame me, I'm neurotic"; "It's my compulsion that does it."

If modern man is not mentally ill, what is he? According to William Glasser, he is *irresponsible* and needs to develop responsibility for himself. According to Eric Berne, he is a *game player*. According to Albert Ellis, he is a *person operating on illogical assumptions*. According to Everett Shostrom, he is first a manipulator who needs to become aware of the manipulative styles of relating to others. Second, he is a person who needs therapeutic goals which are comprehensible and which will motivate and excite him to live his life to its fullest potential. This book attempts to provide a model which meets these two needs.

The troubled person, Shostrom defines as a *manipulator:* a person who exploits, uses, and controls himself and others as "things" in certain identifiable self-defeating ways. The goal of therapy is to become an *actualizor:* a person who appreciates himself and others as *persons* rather than *things,* and who has turned his self-defeating manipulations into self-fulfilling potentials.

I believe that everyone—not just the so-called "sick" or neurotic—can benefit from a diagnosis of his manipulations. This is why Dr. Shostrom's attempt to delineate more clearly a manipulative diagnostic system from my original top-dog/under-dog classification is a useful one.

The purpose of the conventional medical diagnostic system is to determine the appropriate method of treatment. The purpose of the conventional psychiatric diagnostic system, however, cannot be the same, since the technique of psychotherapy is essentially the same, no matter what the psychiatric diagnosis! As Glasser says, "Psychotherapy lacks the specific and individual treatment which follows the diagnosis of scarlet fever, syphillis or malaria." It is my contention, therefore, that a manipulative diagnostic system such as described by Shostrom is much more useful—first, because it represents the reality of manipulative styles of troubled patients; second, because to diagnose the manipulative system of the patient is also to challenge or motivate him toward self-understanding. While medical diagnosis motivates the doctor to make the change, therapeutic diagnosis needs to motivate the patient to change!

The manipulative diagnostic system, from my own experience, does motivate change in the client. In contrast, the traditional psychiatric diagnosis (labeling patients as schizophrenic, compulsive, and so forth) creates morbidity and discouragement in the client when he is made aware of his diagnosis, and creates fear and self-doubt when the diagnosis is not shared with him. Further, such diagnoses sometimes stereotype seriously troubled persons for life.

The simplicity of the manipulative diagnostic system must not cause professional therapists to underrate its significance, for it enables the clinician to diagnose and excite change in any patient seeking therapeutic help. It also moves logically to a goal of actualization and not just to a means of mediocre functioning, which has been for years the sufficient goal of psychiatric therapy.

At the other end of the therapeutic continuum from manipulation is actualization. To Dr. Shostrom's formulations, I would only add that the therapist distinguish between *self*-actualization and self-*concept* actualization. In the former, the patient becomes what he *is*—he discovers his unique identity and then risks being it. The person who tries to become *self-concept actualized* is simply trying to be some phony ideal and not himself.

Two other features of this book which I believe have clinical value are Chapter 4 on Contact, which is a construct having particular significance in Gestalt Therapy, and Chapter 15, which classifies all present systems of therapy into ten dimensions or parameters. I believe that both of these chapters will interest any clinician who is attuned to new developments.

To conclude, I believe that this is a significant book. Laymen and professionals alike will find it interesting and challenging. I believe this book will serve as a layman's guide to many of the principles of Gestalt Therapy. Dr. Shostrom has skillfully interwoven Gestalt Therapy theory into its contents, and I am proud to have been his teacher and therapist.

> Frederick S. Perls, M.D., Ph.D.
> Esalen Institute
> Big Sur, California

PREFACE

Modern man is a manipulator.

He is a used car salesman talking us into an automobile
we wouldn't otherwise buy and a responsible father omnis-
ciently deciding on the college and career for his son. He
is the learned professor drily retailing subject matter with
no opinions of his own, the sunny child cajoling grandpa
to come play in her sandbox, the not-so-dumb blonde
sexily distracting the boss's eye from her bad spelling, and
the bored guest murmuring, "Wonderful party!" when

he could say simply: "Thank you for inviting us." He is
the teen-ager working the adults in his life for the $200
watch he wants for skin diving and the respected businessman driving to success (his own, naturally) on employees
who are, to him, but units of time and talent bought with
a weekly paycheck. Oh, yes, and he is the worker wanting
to know first of all the fringe benefits of the job, not the
skills it may require, and the able-bodied man accepting
a $62.50 unemployment check rather than working for
the $65 he could earn. He is the husband who conceals
his true income from his wife so he can squirrel away a
fund for private pleasures and the good wife who gently
seduces hubby for the new dress he can or cannot afford.
He is the minister preaching in platitudes lest he offend
important parishioners, the aging parent embracing illness as a tool to manipulate the waning attention of busy
sons and daughters, and the politician who promises everything except new taxes.

The manipulator is legion. He is all of us, consciously,
subconsciously, or unconsciously employing all the phoney
tricks we absorb between the cradle and grave to conceal
the actual vital nature of ourselves and, in the process,
reducing ourselves and our fellow man into things to be
controlled.

Not all our manipulating is evil, of course, and some
of it appears necessary in the competitive arena of earning
a livelihood. Much, however, is quite harmful since it
masks real illness which can erupt in shattered lives,
broken marriages, and ruined careers. To the humanistic
psychologist it is tragedy enough that modern man by
his manipulating seems to have lost all his spontaneity, all
capacity to feel and express himself directly and creatively,
thus debasing himself into an anxious automaton who

wastes his hours trying to recapture the past or insure the future. Oh, he talks about his feelings, but he rarely experiences them. He is, in fact, very glib at talking of his troubles and generally quite bad at coping with them, reducing life to a series of verbal and intellectual exercises and drowning himself in a sea of words. He gropes along under a wardrobe of masks and concealing statements, unaware of the real richness of being.

Since this is the first book to deal lengthily with the subject of manipulation, let us define some terms which, while new to the layman, perhaps, are used daily in psychological circles. A *manipulator* may be defined as a person who exploits, uses, and/or controls himself and others as things in certain self-defeating ways. While every man is to some degree a manipulator (I confess), modern humanistic psychology suggests that out of these manipulations we can develop the positive potential which Abraham Maslow and Kurt Goldstein call "self-actualizing." The opposite of the manipulator is the *actualizor* (a rare bird in pure form) who may be defined as a person who appreciates himself and his fellow man as persons or subjects with unique potential—an expresser of his actual self. The paradox is that each of us is partly a manipulator and partly an actualizor, but we can continually become more actualizing.

A person who is *actualizing* trusts his feelings, communicates his needs and preferences, admits to desires and misbehavior, enjoys a worthy foe, offers real help when needed, and is, among many other things, honestly and constructively aggressive. The manipulator, on the other hand, habitually conceals and camouflages his real feelings behind a repertoire of behavior which runs the scale from

15

arrogant hostility to servile flattery in his continuous campaign to serve his own wishes. In part, at least, he is a manipulator because he isn't aware of his actualizing potential. That is one reason for this book—to present the alternative to manipulation and the means for integrating manipulative potentials into actualizing potentials.

I was moved to write it after reading an article, "Man Is Not a Thing," by Erich Fromm, in the March 16, 1957, *Saturday Review*. There Fromm described how today's society centers on the marketplace, where knowledge and manipulation of the customer are of paramount importance. From marketplace manipulation, Fromm pointed out, came a second field of psychology based on the wish to understand and manipulate the employee. It was called "human relations." It was only a step further to harness psychology to manipulate everybody, as in politics.

I propose to explain the alternatives to modern man's manipulations, in the hope that descriptions of the manipulative way of life and the alternative, actualizing way will provide a new direction for living for those who see themselves herein.

A further hope is that this book will help even relatively mature adults to see the manipulations in their lives and to discover alternative actualizing patterns. No book, to be sure, will cure manipulating or magically transmute the reader into an actualizor. Troubled manipulators still will need professional help. However, the hope for the future may exist in professionally guided actualization groups. If they learn to describe themselves accurately, they may help to identify their manipulative devices and spark a desire for richer being. Such groups are forming today, and the book offers them guidelines. Certainly they will see their goals.

16

Preface

To those who may recognize themselves, kinfolk, or friends performing on these pages, it is not enough to say simply: "Be yourself." (Who knows exactly what that might be?) Rather, I like Kierkegaard's affirmation: "To be that self which I truly am." To this I would add, "No matter how foolish, silly, or ridiculous I may be—that's me, and I've got to be patriotic to myself."

To a deeper understanding of this end I address this book.

EVERETT L. SHOSTROM

ACKNOWLEDGMENTS

I would like to thank the following people who have assisted in different ways in the preparation of this manuscript. First of all, Dr. Frederick Perls, my therapist and teacher, the founder of Gestalt Therapy, has provided many ideas on which the concept of manipulation is based.

The work of another valued colleague, Dr. Abraham Maslow, in the area of self-actualization provided the basis for the ideas on the actualization dimension of the book.

Members of the staff of the Institute of Therapeutic Psychology deserve special mention for their continued inspiration and guidance in the preparation of the manuscript. These include Elnora Schmadel, Clara M. D. Riley, Nancy W. Ferry, Richard D. Ferguson, Herbert L. Goodman, Howard Frankl, Lee Bradley, Joanne Morgan, Betty Campbell, and Patti Bannon.

The following people provided material for specific dimensions of the book: Charlotte Spadaro, Patricia Finn, Melissa Meythaler, Gary Herbertson, Maxie Dunnam, James Moothart, John Elder, Theodore Zwemer, Robert Payne, Judy Peterson, Jean Davis, Beulah Van den Beisen, and Dorothy Hufford.

My own children, Connie, Dean, and Dale, were particularly helpful with their ideas for the chapter on adolescence. My wife, Donna, deserves special mention for her patience during the many hours when this manuscript took precedence over family attentions.

I am grateful also to the many patients I have had for the past sixteen years whose experiences provide the core of the examples found in this book. Carolyn Wiens was most helpful with the chapters on children, teen-agers and teaching. I particularly appreciate Dr. James Bugental's critical reading of this manuscript, and I believe his suggestions strengthened the book considerably. Betty Lutes's careful typing of the manuscript and her personal interest and suggestions deserve special thanks. Finally, I wish especially to express my gratitude to John Wesley Noble for putting the technical ideas of this book into conversational style.

CONTENTS

21

PART I

The Human Choice—
Manipulation or Actualization

CHAPTER 1
The Problem

The past half century has brought a deeper understanding
of the processes by which the modern manipulator has
developed.

We know, for example, that the manipulator lacks the
capacity to enjoy himself, to use his knowledge, and to
widen his sense of aliveness and growth. For the manipulator, the understanding of human nature is for just one

purpose: *control*. I am speaking of us all, to one degree or another, you, me, the couple down the block.

Thus the toddling infant soon learns to drool or coo on cue, or have a temper tantrum to get what he wants. His environment thereafter provides constant schooling and ample encouragement in the arts of manipulation. Little wonder then that the teen-ager, who is the modernest of modern men, feeling that life owes him a living and loving and refusing to meet its challenge, brightly picks up the sneaky tricks of control seduction. They are to be found on all sides. Some he absorbs from his father, who plays the responsible parent because he has a secret need for omnipotence, and some from mother, who manipulates desperately to hold onto the apron strings. In the movies the manipulators are the wheeler-dealers. Then there is television, the master instructor, where such as Sergeant Bilko dramatize and glorify the manipulator who can control an army for personal exploitation.

Manipulations are so much a part of our everyday life that the unskilled observer notices only the very obvious or hurtful. They are like birds which are all about us in our natural world. Most of us are fleetingly aware that the birds are there, but save for the common ones, how many of them do we actually identify or describe?

Manipulating, while a particular plague of modern man, is universal, endless, and ageless. We read in the Old Testament in II Samuel, for instance, how David was so smitten with Bathsheba, the beautiful wife of Uriah, that he gave orders for Uriah to be sent into the most dangerous part of the battle, where he would be slain. A gross manipulation. If we read further, we also see how David's latter days were tormented by his guilty love of the lady and then how his handsome, rebellious son "stole the hearts of the men of Israel" and plotted to be king in his father's place. Yes, the ancients manipulated people for control and were themselves manipulated.

The paradox of modern man is that he is an intelligent human being with scientific knowledge of these things, yet permits himself to live in a state of low-grade vitality and unawareness. Generally he does not suffer deeply, but how little he knows of true creative living! What percentage of modern man is like this? Obviously, we don't have a statistic, but it is safe to say that nearly all of us are, to one degree or another. To be sure, we are not all con men, sales "managers," or Elmer Gantry evangelists. Most of us are "just people" doing what comes naturally, but our systems for understanding ourselves haven't been very good.

Man is not born a manipulator. Instead, it is what he learns along the way that makes him troubled or sick, and the tendency to manipulate others, whether it be just a little or a lot, is developed.

Unfortunately for modern man, the common media of learning are weighted fantastically on the side of manipulating. Take our funny friend Bilko. In the years he came into our homes via television, once a week for twenty-two minutes—thirty less eight minutes for the commercial manipulations—how many lessons in manipulating did he teach a generation? And don't forget the reruns. We exalted the guy!

Bilko controlled his army just as the baby controls his parents, the business tycoon his employees and customers, the husband his wife. But Bilko himself was manipulated at times, even if his superiors had to resort to "pulling rank."

Why in the very important matter of raising a boy must

a father pull rank? If he is concerned about his son's friends, for instance, and has stated his honest beliefs, why must he then draw himself up in all his righteous parental robes and thunder, "If you insist on running around with those bums and land in jail, don't come bawling to me for help!" There are hidden reasons for this, as we will see later, but better he should learn to say firmly, "You have judgment, son. Go to jail, if you must, but when you come home, we still will love you because you are our son." That would be better, but it is not likely to happen in the manipulative family circles of modern man. Above all, a manipulator wants no one, not even loved ones, to learn his deeper feelings.

Disguising his true emotions is a hallmark of a manipulator. "My mother died of that," remarks an acquaintance in the matter-of-fact tone of a radio announcer reporting the noon news. This man has come so far in the manipulating role he doesn't actually experience the grief one human being should have naturally for the loss of another, or he is too conditioned to allow himself to express such feelings. From there it's but a short step to having no conscious feelings at all about one's fellow man except as it becomes easier, thereby, to use him as a thing.

In therapy sometimes a person confronts the doctor with the statement: "I'm mad at you." But she is smiling! The therapist learns very early in his career not to trust what a person *says*, as much as what he *is*. He watches the "body language." If she were not a manipulator, she would be *being* what she says she is—angry. Her fists would be clenched, her eyes hot with fury. So the therapist recognizes her statement as a bit of manipulating. The human organism never lies, though his words might.

The manipulator, a poker player with life, strives constantly to conceal his hole card. An example that comes to mind immediately is the professional gambler who actually trains himself to impassivity. (In all our social structure there is no marketplace so manipulative as the legal gaming parlors.) Behind a poker face that only a therapist can penetrate, the gambler may hide his consternation or fury over a huge loss, his gloating over a big win, sometimes even his grief at the death of a trusted and valuable friend or employee. To many modern men this is admirable.

Many people will try to manipulate by requiring that you talk only in their language. For example, there is the super-sanctimonious church elder, who must never, never hear certain objectionable words. Then there are people who use expressions like, "Well, that certainly is interesting," when their eyes show it isn't even remotely interesting to them. What they are trying to do is to be convincing in their interest, without participating. Since the manipulator often is a boaster, my response to reach him must be bluntly penetrating. Sometimes I say simply, "I don't believe you."

Another paradox of the modern manipulator is that while his work offers vast opportunities for enrichment and enjoyment, he does not approach the adventure with either excitement or zest. Hence, he is the anxious automaton refusing to take responsibility for his failures and constantly blaming someone or something else. He goes through a lot of motions, sad tales, and distracting explanations while his body language blabs the truth. Incidentally, while friends may take a long time to recognize the truth, the person who is actualizing will spot the manipulator at once. There is that patent lack of real interest in what he is doing and the give-away facial expressions, whether teen-age pout, poker-faced aloofness, or bland, professional smile. The manipulator, being a phoney, provides the mask he thinks will please the audience and achieve the goal he wants.

His ways of feigning are endless. No doubt you've met the man who quotes Shakespeare at every possible turn of the conversation. He hasn't read more than one of the Bard's plays, but the one he has read, he's almost memorized. This is another tipoff to one type of manipulator: shallow erudition to impress and control. He will go to great lengths to gather just enough learning to take you into his web.

Yet another of the manipulative patterns involves the big businessman with a reputation among his colleagues for the number of secretaries he seduces. The truth of the matter is that he isn't interested in sex, per se. It is the manipulative contest—exerting his power—of getting them to bed that appeals to him. What happens thereafter is often anticlimactic.

Then there is that fellow I call the "Crier." Invariably, when you meet him, he spends the first fifteen minutes giving a recital of how tough things are going in his business whereas the truth may be that things are going very well and he is making a lot of money. The manipulator is one to exaggerate his responsibilities or, conversely, his lack of responsibility.

Some of us quote maxims as if we lived by them. "Always be nice"; "Never offend"; "Don't do anything I wouldn't do" (which can imply many things, but who among us knows another so well we could predetermine what he wouldn't or would do anyway?) ; "Honesty is the best policy"; "The customer is always right." Does anyone really believe the customer is *always* right? And who is always nice and never offends? These are simply more of the empty verbal exercises that manipulators often use.

The person who is *not* manipulating *can* be offended and may say so. He isn't always nice and knows it. The oft-quoted remark of the late Will Rogers that he never met a man he didn't like might bring a smile to his face and the gentle rejoinder: "Well, I guess old Will just didn't meet some of the people I do." You see, he views life as it really *is,* and if superficial maxims disturb him, it's because he understands human nature for what it is. Usually he has more immediate things to absorb his attention.

The manipulator, on the other hand, thinks of his activities as bothersome chores to be got out of the way. He knows little of how to contact and savor the moment or how to experience his deeper feelings. He feels that the time for fun and pleasure, for growing and learning is childhood and youth. When he reaches "maturity," he abdicates life. In this state he is truly vegetating without any awareness of his existence.

Abraham Lincoln, in so many ways the Great Emancipator, left us a cogent lesson when he spoke at New Salem, Illinois, after being defeated in his early try for Congress. "If the good people, in their wisdom, shall see fit to keep me in the background," he said, "I have been too familiar with disappointments to be very much chagrined." He accepted that every race has both a winner and loser, and losing, he went into training for the next try.

How different is the reaction of the manipulator who fails to win the promotion or pay raise he has set his heart upon. By the time he gets home, he has managed to shift the blame to his long-dead father for dominating him, or to his wife for failing to cook his eggs right that morning. He may now get drunk or sick, turn servile toady or sulkily go on a passive strike aganst himself, mankind, and his unreasonable boss. He may even just blank out and let someone else have his place by default.

Parallel to the need *to control* is the manipulator's need *to be controlled*. For centuries man has attempted to solve the riddle by resorting to a system of *moralistic control* utilizing the concepts of "good" and "bad." He has sought some authority to decide for him what was good and what was bad. The paradox, of course, is that this leads to the definition of "good" being that which pleases authority and "bad" being that which displeases authority. More importantly, the moralistic concepts of good and bad lead to a psychology of *rejection,* since the individual must decide which parts of himself are good and try to be those parts, and then try to decide which are bad and reject or deny those. A little reflection leads to the conclusion that these decisions create a continuous civil war inside the individual—he never is quite sure what is good and what is bad.

There is an alternative to this which may be described as *natural control.* A solution of rejection for controlling human behavior will never work. All human tendencies need to be respected. You wouldn't cut off your left arm and try to use only your right, nor would you try to amputate any part of your personality. However, since each side of the self can be expressed either unwisely or creatively, the problem becomes one of choice and responsibility. Freedom in this sense, then, is the choice and responsibility taken for the style in which an individual expresses himself. This approach is not one of rejection or doing away with part of the personality, but rather one of becoming aware of what occurs when we do express ourselves in self-defeating ways.

I would define *self-defeating behavior* as manipulative behavior and *creative behavior* as actualizing behavior. *Actualizing behavior is simply manipulative behavior expressed more creatively.* We are all manipulators, but rather than reject our manipulative behavior, we should try to transform or modify it into actualizing behavior. Nothing in ourselves needs to be rejected in order to do this.

I believe that in each of us there are two sides, which Frederick Perls calls the "top-dog" and the "under-dog." Top-dog is the active side in that it is more energetic, commanding, and authoritative. The under-dog is the passive side in that it is compliant and submissive. Each of these sides can be expressed in either a manipulative or a creative, actualizing way.

Manipulation has no necessary relationship to, or usefulness in, authentic living. In reality, much of the manipulator's dissatisfaction with himself and his world stems from the fact that while he has swallowed many of the terms and concepts of modern psychiatry and psychology, he has not tested them or used his verbal ability and intellectual knowledge as tools of power they are supposed to be. Too often he uses psychological concepts as rationalizations, ways of perpetuating unsatisfactory behavior. The manipulator justifies current unhappiness by past experiences and wallows in his misery. He uses his knowledge of man as an excuse for socially destructive and self-destructive behavior. Though he has graduated from the infant's "I can't (help myself)," it has been only to the adult's "I can't help myself *because* . . . I'm too shy *or* I am introverted *or* my mother rejected me." Because, because, because. . . !

Psychology never was meant to be a justification for

continuing manipulative behavior—behavior that does not permit the individual to live up to the maximum of his potential. The aim of psychology is not merely to offer explanations of behavior. It is to help us arrive at self-knowledge, fulfillment, and self-support.

Having considered the phenomenon in general terms, let us now get to specifics and look a little closer at this manipulator in us all.

CHAPTER 2
The Manipulator

A manipulator is a person who exploits, uses, or controls himself and others as "things" in self-defeating ways. I would say further that the modern manipulator has developed from our "scientific" emphases as well as from our marketplace orientation, which sees man as a thing to know about, to influence, and to manipulate.

Erich Fromm has said that things can be dissected or

manipulated without damage to their nature, but man is not a thing.[1] He cannot be dissected without being destroyed; he cannot be manipulated without being harmed. Yet the very objective of the marketplace is to achieve this "thingness" in people!

Here, man is no longer a man but a customer. To the sales manager he is a prospect, to the tailor a suit, to the bond salesman a bank account; even at the beauty parlor, which performs a rather intimate personal service, madame is a generality, "the patron." All of this tends to depersonalize us and deprive us of our individuality, and we resent it. I don't want to be a "head" to my barber; I want to be Everett Shostrom, a live and vibrant person. We all want particularity, but that is not what we have when we're hooked by systems of commercial thought which tend to destroy that very quality. When the con artists of the selling game cajole us with stock phrases, meaning not a bit of it, we resent it, and them.

Since there is some of the manipulator in all of us, let's see if we can't bring him into clearer focus. I would say that there are some fundamental types of manipulators, as illustrated in Figure 1. Paradoxically, Figure 1 is a picture of a typical therapy group and also a picture of each of us with our various self-defeating manipulative techniques. Let me describe each of them:

1. The *Dictator* exaggerates his strength. He dominates, orders, quotes authorities, and does anything that will control his victims. Variations of the Dictator are the Mother Superiors, Father Superiors, the Rank Pullers, the Boss, the Junior Gods.

2. The *Weakling* is usually the Dictator's victims, the polar opposite. The Weakling develops great skill in

Figure 1
The Manipulative Types[2]

coping with the Dictator. He exaggerates his sensitivity. He forgets, doesn't hear, is passively silent. Variations of the Weakling are the Worrier, the "Stupid-Like-a-Fox," the Giver-Upper, the Confused, the Withdrawer.

3. The *Calculator* exaggerates his control. He deceives, lies, and constantly tries to outwit and control other people. Variations of the Calculator are the High-pressure Salesman, the Seducer, the Poker Player, the Con Artist, the Blackmailer, the Intellectualizor.

4. The *Clinging Vine* is the polar opposite of the Calculator. He exaggerates his dependency. He is the person who wants to be led, fooled, taken care of. He lets others do his work for him. Variations of the Clinging Vine are the Parasite, the Crier, the Perpetual Child, the Hypochondriac, the Attention Demander, the Helpless One.

5. The *Bully* exaggerates his aggression, cruelty and unkindness. He controls by implied threats of some kind. He is the Humiliator, the Hater, the Tough Guy, the Threatener. The female variation is the Bitch or Nagger.

6. The *Nice Guy* exaggerates his caring, love, and kills with kindness. In one sense, he is much harder to cope with than the Bully. You can't fight a Nice Guy! Curiously, in any conflict with the Bully, Nice Guy almost always wins! Variations of the Nice Guy are the Pleaser, the Nonviolent One, the Nonoffender, the Noninvolved One, the Virtuous One, the Never-Ask-for-What-You-Want One, the Organization Man.

7. The *Judge* exaggerates his criticalness. He distrusts everybody and is blameful, resentful, slow to forgive. Variations of the Judge are the Know-It-All, the Blamer, the Deacon, the Resentment Collector, the Shoulder, the Shamer, the Comparer, the Vindicator, the Convictor.

8. The *Protector* is the opposite of the Judge. He exaggerates his support and is nonjudgmental to a fault. He spoils others, is over-sympathetic, and refuses to allow those he protects to stand up and grow up for themselves. Instead of caring for his own needs, he cares only for others' needs. Variations of the Protector are the Mother Hen, the Defender, the Embarrassed-for-Others, the Fearful-for-Others, the Sufferer-for-Others, the Martyr, the Helper, the Unselfish One.

The manipulator over exaggerates any one or combination of these types. Usually when we are most strongly one type, we project its opposite onto others around us, making them our targets. Weakling wife, for instance, often chooses a husband who is a Dictator and then controls him by her subversive devices.

So each of us, paradoxically, is such a group, with all these manipulative potentials, and any therapeutic group is each of us turned inside out! This is why, as we shall see later, group therapy is so effective in helping the manipulator to see himself in others. The reason we seem different to different people is that we expose only certain manipulations to some and other manipulations to others. This is the reason that we must be careful not to judge another by other peoples' opinions, for, too often, they have seen only certain sides of the person.

Causes of Manipulation

I would agree with Frederick Perls that a basic cause for manipulation lies in man's eternal conflict between self-support and environmental support. There is a good deal of this in employer-employee relationships. The employer, for example, creates the sales manual (a dastardly thing!) as a substitute for individual thinking. He patently does

39

not trust the individual salesman to approach the customer with his own individuality, to size him up, and then to *be* what comes naturally. Instead, the salesman must make his approach within the limited framework of the pre-fabbed manual of thought provided by the boss and thus receives insult to his personal integrity and, in turn, is an insult to the customer.

The employee in our modern society, on the other hand, tends to be a freeloader, a fringe-benefit-getter. He demands certain rights and privileges without having made an effort to demonstrate his ability and performance. I had a firsthand example of this not long ago while interviewing an applicant for work to be done on a small commercial project. He wasn't at all interested in showing me what he could contribute; instead, he first demanded a contract. With it he wanted participation in the profits although he hadn't been part of the project at its beginning.

Not trusting himself for self-support, man believes his salvation lies in trusting others. Yet, not trusting the other person completely, modern man manipulates the other in an effort to support himself in the process. It is as if he rides the coattail of the other person and then attempts to steer him at the same time; or, to use a more modern analogy, he is the backseat driver refusing to drive, yet driving the driver! The word that describes this cause of manipulation is "distrust." We cannot really *trust* the natural organismic balance each of us has, which would allow us to live our lives simply and feelingly. In great part this is a fruit of childhood, in which we are taught that our organism is like a wild horse which we must ride and never let go of, which we must control vigilantly.

Erich Fromm has suggested a second cause for manipulation in modern man. He reasons that the ultimate relationship between man and man is that of love, and that love is knowing a human being as he is and loving his ultimate essence. The world's great religions admonish us to love our neighbor as we would ourselves, but here unfortunately, we run into an operational snag. How many people know how? Most aren't even aware that we can't love our neighbor *until we love ourselves.*

We seem to assume that the more perfect we appear—the more flawless—the more we will be loved. Actually, the reverse is more apt to be true. The more willing we are to admit our weaknesses as human beings, the more lovable we are. Nevertheless, love is an achievement not easy to attain, and thus the alternative that the manipulator has is a desperate one—that of complete power over the other person, the power that makes him do what *we* want, feel what *we* want, think what *we* want, and which transforms him into a thing, *our* thing.

A third suggestion for the causes of manipulation is posed by James Bugental and the existentialists. Risk and contingency, they point out, are on every side of us, as though our every act were a stone dropped in a pond. The number and potentialities of the things that may happen to us at any minute are beyond our knowing. Modern man feels powerless when he faces this existential situation. According to Bugental, the *passive manipulator* says, " 'Since I can't control everything that will determine what happens to me, I have no control at all.' Experiencing the unpredictability of his life, the patient gives up and enacts this feeling of having no possibility of affecting what happens to him. He makes himself totally an object." [3] The passive manipulator thereupon lapses into an inertia which accentuates his helplessness. To the layman it might appear that the passive manipulator now becomes automatically a victim of the active manipulator. Not so. This is a sneaky trick of the passive manipulator. As Perls has shown, in any encounter between top dog and under dog in life, the under dog most always wins. An example of this is the mother who gets sick because she can't handle her children. Her helplessness causes them to become subservient to some degree and to give in, even though they don't want to.

The *active manipulator,* on the other hand, "victimizes other people, capitalizing on their powerlessness, and apparently gaining gratification by exercising gratuitous control over them. Parents who are oppressed by the dread of powerlessness often need to make their children excessively dependent upon them and to defeat the child's efforts to gain independence." [4] Usually the parent is the top dog and the child the under dog, and we see the use of the "If-Then" technique. *"If* you eat your potatoes, then you may watch television." *"If* you do your homework, then you may use the car." Naturally the modern child soon learns the technique too. "If I mow the lawn, then how much do I get?" "If Jim's father lets him use the car every weekend, then why can't I?"

The truly active manipulator might simply roar: "Do as I say and no questions!" We see it in business: "I own fifty-one percent of the stock, and they will wear this uniform because *I* want them to." Even in education. The founder of the college where I once taught used to say: "I don't care what color the buildings are, so long as they are blue."

A fourth possible cause for manipulation is suggested in the writings of Jay Haley, Eric Berne, and William Glasser. Haley, in his work with schizophrenics, has found that the schizophrenic is intensively afraid of close *interpersonal relationships* and so tries to avoid such relationships. Berne suggests that people play games in order to regulate their emotions and thereby avoid *intimacy*. Glasser suggests that one of the basic fears of people is their fear of *involvement*. In effect, then, a manipulator is a person who ritualistically relates to people in an effort to avoid intimacy or involvement.

A fifth suggested cause for manipulation comes from the work of Albert Ellis. He writes that each of us learns, in the process of growing up, certain illogical assumptions about living. One of them is that it is a dire necessity to be approved by *everyone*.[5] The passive manipulator, Ellis suggests, is a person who refuses to be truthful and honest with others and instead tries to please everyone because he is basing his life on this foolish assumption.

Games vs. Manipulation

It should be made clear that when I refer to manipulation I mean something more than "playing games," as developed in Berne's *Games People Play*. First, manipulation is a *system* of games or a *style of life,* as opposed merely to *playing* an individual game to avoid involvement with another person. Manipulation is more akin to what Berne refers to as "a script," which is a recurrent pattern of games that characterizes a lifetime system of dealing with people. Secondly, the manipulator uses games along with other maneuvers to exploit or control *himself* as well as others. Thirdly, manipulation is a pseudo-philosophy of life, not just a trick. As we proceed, these distinctions

43

between game playing and manipulation will be seen more clearly.

For instance, Weakling Wife, the manipulator, has turned her whole existence into a subtle campaign to make her Dictator Husband responsible for her life's woes. To some extent, this pattern exists in most marriages, yours and mine included, although the roles may be reversed. Berne, on the other hand, by pinpointing her individual games, such as "Kick Me," "Harried," "Look How Hard I've Tried," and "Now I've Got You, You S.O.B.," helps us to understand her modus operandi. After she has seduced him into kicking and abusing her, she tries to convince him he is a louse for having done it. Her manipulative system, which is bigger than the sum of all the games, may be called "injustice collecting."

A rather attractive young lady of twenty-five, bleached blonde and shapely, sat in my office one day. She hoped to impress me with the fact that she was "a nice girl"—the feminine counterpart of the Nice Guy manipulator—and that she was constantly having to fight off attempts by men (the Bullies in her life) of making improper advances. I observed the low-cut dress, the high-riding hemline, and the green light in her glance. In her story I recognized that she habitually had played what Berne calls the "Rapo" game with men many times, but what I really saw was a life-style of flirtations followed by rejections when the man rose to the bait. She was, of course, denying the Bully in herself. She was winning every encounter, not losing it, as she was implying. Her hostility was expressed in her naïveté, and she refused to admit it. The object of therapy would be to help her recognize her Bully and then use both her strength and weakness to quit playing this continuing manipulative system of "seek-and-go-hide."

Summary of Manipulative Systems

A manipulative system may be described as a pattern of manipulations or games. At this writing, there appear to be four basic types:

1. The *active* manipulator attempts to control others by active methods. He avoids facing his own weaknesses by assuming the role of the powerful one in a relationship. Usually he does this with some institutional affiliation or rank (parent, top sergeant, teacher, boss). He plays "top dog" and gains gratification but capitalizes on others' feelings of powerlessness to gain control over them. He uses such techniques as creating obligations and expectations, pulling rank, pushing people around like puppets.

2. The *passive* manipulator is the reverse of the active. He decides, since he cannot control life, that he will give up and allow the active manipulator to control him. He feigns helplessness and stupidity and plays the "under dog." Whereas the active manipulator wins by winning, the passive manipulator, paradoxically, wins by losing. By allowing the active manipulator to do his thinking and work for him, in a sense, he wins out over the top dog by his passivity and deadness.

3. The *competitive* manipulator sees life as a constant game of winning and losing in which he has to be the vigilant fighter. To him, life is a battle, and all others are competitors or enemies, real or potential. He sees all men as "racing dogs" in the game of life. He alternates between top-dog- and under-dog methods and so may be seen as somewhat of a mixture between the active and passive manipulator.

4. A fourth basic form of the manipulative system is that of *indifferent manipulation*. The manipulator plays hopeless, indifferent to, and withdraws from his contact with another. His stock phrase is "I don't care." He treats the other as if he were dead—a puppet who has lost the capacity for growth and change. His methods are also both active and passive, sometimes playing the Nagger, Bitch, or Martyr, or Helpless. His secret, of course, is that he still cares and has not given up, or he would not continue to play the manipulative game. Husbands and wives often play this game with each other. As one treats the other like a puppet, the attitude of indifference creates a puppetlike quality in himself. This is why the system is self-defeating. The "Divorce Threatening Game" is an example by which the manipulator secretly hopes to win back his partner, rather than to truly separate from him.

Having now examined the philosophy and systems of the manipulator, we see more clearly that he always regards himself and others as objects. The basic philosophy of the active manipulator is to maintain control at all costs; of the passive manipulator, never to offend; of the competitive manipulator, to win at all costs; and of the indifferent manipulator, to deny caring. Obviously, the manipulator can never be himself, nor can he ever relax because his system of games and maneuvers requires that he always play a role rather than be himself.

Turning next to an examination of the actualizor, we will see a suggested system or philosophy of life which pays greater dividends in the living. Again there must be a caution that a book can only be like the white line down the road on a foggy night. To change over from manipulating to actualizing requires having some kind of experience and, unfortunately—and perhaps sounding a little like

Gertrude Stein—an experience is not an experience unless you experience it.

Even then, the ways of human nature aren't always predictable. I think of a story I heard recently about a small town little theater group which got down to its last member in casting a play. He wasn't much of an actor but the part called only for a walk-on, when a gun would fire and he had his single line: "My God, I am shot!" Alas, the man wasn't quite up to it. No matter how many times they rehearsed, the line came out rigidly mechanical. He wasn't *experiencing* the shock of a bullet. The director decided finally on a ruse. He would load the gun secretly with rock salt, hoping that when it hit, the wooden actor would "feel" his role. Came the night of the performance and the duffer's scene. He walked on, the gun fired, the rock salt stung. Then he saw blood. "My God!" he shrieked, "I really *am* shot!"

But of course that wasn't the line.

Notes

1. See Erich Fromm, "Man Is Not a Thing," *Saturday Review,* March 16, 1957, pp. 9-11.

2. The internal dimensions of this figure are adapted from Timothy Leary, *The Interpersonal Theory of Personality* (New York: The Ronald Press Company, 1957).

3. J. F. T. Bugental, *The Search for Authenticity* (New York: Holt, Rinehart & Winston, 1965), p. 298.

4. *Ibid.,* p. 299.

5. Albert Ellis, "New Approaches to Psychotherapy," *Journal of Clinical Psychology, Monograph Supplement,* 1955, p. 11.

CHAPTER 3
The Actualizor

I promised at the outset that a purpose of this book would
be to show the alternatives to manipulation and to point
out some of the ways in which one becomes "more patriotic
to himself." Here it might be well to elaborate on the
concept of actualization. The term derives from what
Abraham Maslow has called the "self-actualizing person,"

one who is functioning more fully than the average individual and thereby is living a more enriched life.

His life is enriched because he is using all the potentials available to him. Too often man is so busy trying to exert control over others that he doesn't see or hear what is all about him. He isn't free to do all that life offers him or to relish all his resources for living. Manipulating steals him blind. Oh, the manipulator may *talk* about sunsets and such, but only because he thinks that he should. He may, in fact, dowse them in his ocean of words, but they are *only* words. He doesn't *experience* them, and he can't truly enjoy them. He isn't sick necessarily (though he may be); he's just too busy. It is to reach him, in part, that modern psychology is taking its new, humanistic approach.

In the past, psychologists believed that we best could understand psychological health by first understanding psychological illness. Again Maslow suggests the alternative viewpoint. He teaches that we can understand psychological health by studying the lives of those people who *have achieved* a high degree of self-satisfaction or fulfillment—the healthy champions, as it were—and it is largely from his research that our understanding of these people comes. Maslow's approach has been to study those unusual people who have demonstrated self-actualization—the self-actualiz*ed* person.

While a mere one percent of mankind has been selected as fully self-actualized by Maslow's estimate, it should encourage the rest of us to note that an ever-increasing number, through psychotherapy, self-understanding, religious experience, or education, today can become self-actualiz*ing*—can be *on the way,* even though they haven't arrived.

Fundamental Characteristics

A manipulator's style of life involves four fundamental characteristics: deception, unawareness, control, and cynicism. The actualizor's philosophy of life is marked by four opposing characteristics: honesty, awareness, freedom, and trust. (See Table 1.) The change from manipulation to actualization is in general on a continuum *from* deadness and deliberateness *to* aliveness and spontaneity.

Table 1
Fundamental Characteristics of Manipulators and Actualizors Contrasted

Manipulators	*Actualizors*
1. Deception (Phoniness, Knavery). The manipulator uses tricks, techniques, and maneuvers. He puts on an act, plays roles to create an *impression*. His expressed feelings are deliberately chosen to fit the occasion.	1. Honesty (Transparency, Genuineness, Authenticity). The actualizor is able honestly to be his feelings, whatever they may be. He is characterized by candidness, *expression,* and genuinely being himself.
2. Unawareness (Deadness, Boredom). The manipulator is unaware of the really important concerns of living. He has "Tunnel	2. Awareness (Responsiveness, Aliveness, Interest). The actualizor fully looks and listens to himself and others. He is fully aware of nature, art,

Vision." He sees only what he wishes to see and hears only what he wishes to hear.

music, and the other real dimensions of living.

3. Control (Closed, Deliberate).
The manipulator plays life like a game of chess. He appears relaxed, yet is very controlled and controlling, concealing his motives from his "opponent."

3. Freedom (Spontaneity, Openness).
The actualizor is spontaneous. He has the freedom to be and express his potentials. He is master of his life, a subject and not a puppet or object.

4. Cynicism (Distrust).
The manipulator is basically distrusting of himself and others. Down deep he doesn't trust human nature. He sees relationships with humans as having two alternatives: to control or *be* controlled.

4. Trust (Faith, Belief).
The actualizor has a deep trust in himself and others to relate to and and cope with life in the here and now.

Certainly our go-go society, in which the marketplace orientation is overwhelmingly apparent, makes actualizing difficult. Consider the businessman, who may not even make an attempt to become an actualizor until a sudden heart attack causes him to ponder what life really is about. Prior to that, he is too busy. The first half of life, Carl

Jung points out, deals with achievement, getting an education and job, and marrying, while the second half is when the inner self develops. If it doesn't, Jung warns, the individual will surely get sick, for the rules for the afternoon of life are not those for the morning of life.

The Differences Between Manipulative and Actualizing Relationships

An actualizor is an appreciator of his own uniqueness. Martin Buber has expressed it as follows:

Every person born into this world represents something new, something that never existed before, something original and unique. "It is the duty of every person . . . to know and consider that he is unique in the world in his particular character and that there has never been anyone like him in the world, for if there had been someone like him, there would have been no need for him to be in the world. Every single man is a new thing in the world, and is called upon to fulfill his particularity in this world. . . ." Every man's foremost task is the actualization of his unique, unprecedented and never recurring potentialities, and not the repetition of something that another, and be it even the greatest, has already achieved.[1]

Buber has described the contrast between a manipulative and an actualizing relationship as the difference between an "I-It" and "I-Thou" relationship. I would go one step further and say that a manipulative relationship is an "It-It" relationship, and an actualizing relationship is a "Thou-Thou" relationship. This is an important difference, since it suggests that the person who regards another as a "thou" also becomes a "thou," and the person who regards another as an "it" becomes an "it."

Appreciation of each other comes about through expres-

sion: each one expressing wants or needs instead of demanding, each expressing preferences instead of ordering,
each expressing acceptance of each other rather than
tolerance, and each even being willing to genuinely
surrender to each other's wishes instead of "playing submissive." The relationship is one of closeness, as opposed
to one of distance.

Thus, the actualizor, in effect, may be called an appreciator of himself and others as "thou's" or valued human
beings, as opposed to "its" or "things" connected with the
manipulator.

Man has many actualizing potentials. Some we come to
appreciate or value more than others. The more we can
appreciate *all* actualizing aspects or sides of ourselves, the
more fully actualizing we become. The more sides of ourselves that we find *un*valuable, the more we feel like an
"it" and need to be a manipulator and see others as "its"
or "things."

Thus, the manipulator feels *un*appreciated. The more
he disvalues himself the more of himself he must project
or disown and treat as "things" outside himself. When we
do something that we dislike, we say: "It came over me,"
or *"That's* not like me." Soon this tendency to disown or
deny spreads into all areas of our lives. When the home
team is losing, it is no longer "our team" but "that team"
or "them bums." Similarly, one's sweetheart becomes
"the nag" or "the ball and chain" Hubby becomes the
"meal ticket" or the "dictator." When you feel like an "it,"
others about you seem like "its" too.

When you are actualizing, you appreciate yourself and
others, and you don't need to manipulate others to control
them. You operate from a position of *self-worth* rather

than from a position of *deficiency*. Seeing yourself as a "thou" of worth, you will also see others as "thous."

The manipulator operates from the assumption that his deficiency can only be overcome by *fighting* himself and those around him. To him, life is a battle with strategy, tactics, tricks, or games necessary for survival. When he loses a battle or contest, he feels he has lost everything. The actualizor sees life not as a battle, but as a growth process with appreciation coming naturally with self-development.

Here I must make what is perhaps the most important statement of this book: *While the manipulator is a many-faceted person of antagonistic opposites, the actualizor is a many-faceted person of complimentary opposites.*

Figure 2 shows the actualizing person as a combination of four complimentary potentials, all developed usually out of former manipulative potentials. You may not agree with the choice of examples, whose lives demonstrated these potentials in certain ways. Perhaps you can choose your own candidates.

1. From the Dictator develops the Leader. The Leader leads rather than dictates. He is forceful, yet not dominating. An example of an actualizing Leader in history is Winston Churchill. Through the World War II years he exemplified leadership of the greatest democratic type.

The complimentary opposite of the Leader is the Empathizer. The Empathizer not only talks, but listens and is aware of his weaknesses. He demands good work, yet accepts the human tendency to err. Such a person was Eleanor Roosevelt. She knew her personal limitations and empathized with the underdeveloped nations and peoples of the world in her work with the United Nations.

Figure 2

The Actualizing Types

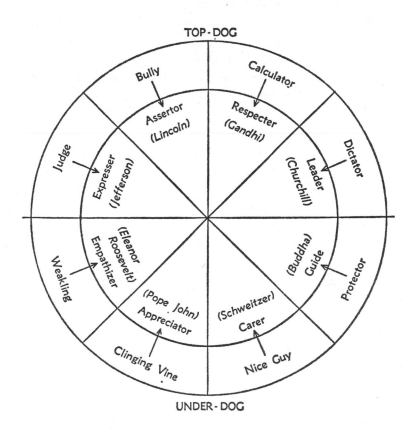

TOP-DOG

Bully

Calculator

Assertor
(Lincoln)

Respecter
(Gandhi)

Judge

Expresser
(Jefferson)

Leader
(Churchill)

Dictator

(Eleanor
Roosevelt)
Empathizer

(Buddha)
Guide

Weakling

Protector

(Pope John)
Appreciator

(Schweitzer)
Carer

Clinging Vine

Nice Guy

UNDER-DOG

The actualizor integrates both his leadership and em-pathy. A person who demonstrated such integration was Adlai Stevenson in his ability to stand firm in the United Nations and at the same time to tune sensitively into all the voices of the world.

2. From the Calculator develops the Respecter. Rather than using or exploiting, the actualizor respects himself and others as "thous" rather than "things." Such a person was Mahatma Gandhi. This man in his nonviolence always deeply respected those with whom he dealt.

The complimentary opposite of the Respecter is the Appreciator. The Appreciator does not simply depend on others, but appreciates the different skills that others have to offer. He appreciates different points of view from his own and does not need to have other people think the same as he thinks. Pope John XXIII illustrates the Appreciator in his ambassadorship with other world religions.

The actualizor integrates both his respect and appreciation. Such an integration we see in the great Jewish theologian, Martin Buber. To him, each person was unique, irreplaceable, particular, and not the repetition of any other. He saw others as "thous."

3. From the Bully develops the Assertor. The Assertor enjoys a worthy foe, but he is direct and straightforward. He is not hostile and dominating as is the Bully. Abraham Lincoln showed this characteristic in the famous Lincoln-Douglas debates as well as in his leadership during the Civil War.

The complimentary opposite of the Assertor is the Carer. The Carer is not the obsequious Nice Guy, but is affectionate, friendly, and deeply loving. Albert Schweitzer, in his deep devotion to the African people showed this characteristic.

The actualizor integrates both his assertion and caring. He is strong in his interpersonal relations and yet has the capacity for caring contact. He integrates aggression with tenderness. John F. Kennedy in his handling of the Cuban crisis showed such assertion, and yet one is reminded of his tender devotion to his children.

4. From the Judge develops the Expresser. The expresser is not judgmental of others, but is able to express his own convictions strongly. Thomas Jefferson showed this characteristic in his writings.

The complimentary opposite of the Expresser is the Guide. The Guide does not protect or teach others, but gently helps each person to find his own way. Buddha, the founder of the great Eastern religion, was such a man. His dictum was that each man must find "the way" up the mountain for himself.

The actualizor integrates both his expression and guidance. He does not think *for* others but *with* them. He helps others help themselves by his own expression of views and yet gives each the right to make his own decisions. The Sermon on the Mount was deeply expressive, and yet the Beatitudes were *invitations,* not demands. Such was the actualizing nature of Jesus.

Achieving Integration

Perhaps the most important thing to understand from the foregoing discussion is that an individual may be compared to a two-party system in politics or may be like a battery with positive and negative poles. The actualizor is developed from the integration of manipulative poles. A simple example illustrates: An individual feels lonely.

Therapist: Be your lonesome self. (Weakling)

Patient: I feel so blue and unhappy; I just need people.

Therapist: Now be your strong opposite self. (Dictator)

Patient: Oh, quit being such a weakling. You know that you don't need anybody else but me.

Therapist:	Now be the weak one again.
Patient:	What good are you?
Therapist:	Now be the strong one and answer.
Patient:	Without me you're a machine with only one wheel, but with me we drive the machine together.
Therapist:	Now be the weak one and answer.
Patient:	Gosh, I never thought of that. I guess we can be strong when we work together.

The above is an example of an individual *listening to* both sides of himself, both "weak" (under dog) and "strong" (top dog). Through the conflict, antagonistic poles become complementary. When both sides of ourselves are accepted, this leads to the power of integration.

Imperfections of Self-Actualized People

The mistake most people make is to think that the self-actualized person is a superhuman person with no weaknesses. The truth is that he very often is silly, wasteful, or thoughtless and can be thoroughly stubborn or irritating.

What I want to make clear is that the self-actualized person is an exciting person and not a stuffed shirt or joyless person, as many might want to make him. His virtues are extraordinary, but his faults are also very much present.

So as one becomes his actualizing potentials, it is important not to seek perfection but to discover the joy that comes from integration of both strength and weaknesses —to freely skate between all potentials.

1. Martin Buber, *The Way of Man* (Chicago: Wilcox and Follett, 1951), p. 16.

Part II
The Goals of Actualization

CHAPTER 4

Contact vs. Manipulation

An actualizing relationship between two people is one individual's relating himself to another core-to-core. By "core," we mean the inner range of potentials. This inner core may also be called one's real, authentic, or actualizing self.

Through expressing his various passive and active potentials, such as caring and assertiveness, the actualizor opens paths for spontaneous "understanding" of himself, as well as others. He doesn't look upon other persons as objects, but "touches" them, at the same time retaining and enhancing his own selfhood. Very good friends, as we know, are said to communicate their "sensitivity" to each other. This is contact. A wife may contact her husband through a smile or a sigh if it is core-to-core.

In order to understand the difference between contact and manipulation, see Figure 3. Contact is shown as the touching of two inner cores of actualizing potentials. Manipulation is shown as communication between the two peripheries of outer rings of the personalities of two individuals. It can be seen from these diagrams that contact is a form of loving or trusting another person in a relationship of closeness or touching, whereas manipulation is a relationship to distance that represents a withdrawal to less personal or intense forms of communication.

Contact is not a permanent state; instead, it is a fragile thing which must be developed at each meeting. When contact exists, we express ourselves and feel *listened to* rather than impressing someone else and merely *hearing* them. Our own words come easily and expressively. The paradox of human behavior is that while personal contact is said to be highly valued in our lives, it is rare and difficult to establish—with most people, that is. It is not rare in actualizing persons.

All manipulative expressions create loss of contact since they represent withdrawal from core expression. (See again Figure 3.) Just when you feel you're about to get on a meaningful contact level with someone, your husband, for instance, he manages to break the connection. He may say (being judgmental), "I don't think you have any call to say that." Then he's safely out of actualizing contact.

62

Figure 3
Contact vs. Manipulation

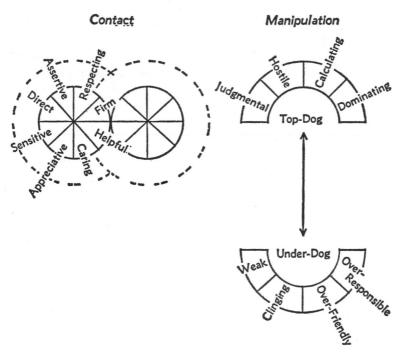

Contact is shown as communication between the two inner cores of actualizing potentials of two individuals. Each person is being his full actualizing potentials in intimate contact.

Manipulation is shown as communication between the two outer rings of the personalities of two individuals. The top dog emphasizes the active extremes; the under dog emphasizes the passive extremes. The relationship is not intimate but distant.

Another example: A man and wife may be talking about their children, and she says: "It seems to me you're not close to your daughter." If pursued, this line of talk might lead to a vital and valuable discussion, for this man *is* afraid of expressing a sense of caring for his daughter. He was controlled so by his mother that he is afraid of closeness to women in general. Being hostile, he retorts, "You're the one who's not close!" and breaks it off. Then he adds: "By the way, I'd like to talk about that weekend she's planning and if we ought to let her go." Rather than get into a core-to-core discussion of feelings, which might reveal his fear of caring for his daughter, he changes the topic in order to talk intellectually about her activities.

One reason for a manipulator's inability to sustain contact is fear of vulnerability, exposure, and of being judged. He fears sustained contact will reveal a core dimension of himself which has heretofore been denied, or which he has refused to see. In the above example, the father was afraid to show his caring potential.

True personal contact involves *risk*. The manipulator chooses instead to *control* those around him. For example, the father above says of his daughter's planned weekend: "I won't let her go!" becoming dominating. He avoids saying what really is on his mind: "I'm afraid she might get seduced." He is denying his core caring for her as he might express it if he were in contact with her. He even tries to calculate reasons. Rather than acknowledging, "Well, I can see it from her viewpoint, but—," he says, "I'm just not going to allow her to go. She might get snowed in up there." Or, "Girls shouldn't be away from home that long." At no point will he reveal his true caring for her.

The manipulator *must* control conversations. He chooses the topic, evaluates rather than listens, tries to convince rather than appreciates, or he may limit the talk to conventional remarks on "safe" subjects like the weather. In other people such generalities may be a prelude to contact, but in the manipulator, more often than not, they are only a means of avoiding personal contact.

Jay Haley suggests several means by which the manipulator may control communication: [1]

By denying that he is communicating. "I think you should apologize to him, but it's not my place to tell you." (He has said it but at the same time denies that he has.) Having said something, he may blame "liquor" or "my sick headache" or contend that "they" said it.

By denying the message itself. "Oh, forget it"; "I guess it wasn't important." Or he insists the message is misunderstood: "You didn't get the point."

By denying that the message is communicated to the other person. "I was just talking to myself"; "Just thinking out loud. . . ."

By denying the context or situation. "You always make fun of me" (referring to the past) ; or "You will think I'm silly" (referring to the future) . In both examples he avoids dealing with the other person *now*.

Core Relationships Vs. Casual Relationships

A contact relationship is one in which the participants have developed sufficient security and openness to contact one another deeply. Love or caring may be defined, in fact, as liking plus openness plus contact. Obviously, not many relationships could be maintained at this level since contacting takes time and energy, and most relationships, therefore, must be casual and superficial. Nevertheless, without one or two meaningful contact relationships, an individual cannot be fulfilled, nor can he reach his actualizing potential.

Contact Vs. Withdrawal

Most of us have a feeling of what it is to be touched by another person or situation, but the nature of this experi-

ence is not usually clear. Often we find ourselves withdrawing from people and situations, and we feel guilty
about this withdrawal, not understanding that it can be
healthy. You don't want to go to the party to which you
have been invited Saturday night; your wife has said you
should go. You even feel guilty about leaving a party early
when the people don't interest you or guilty about wanting
to terminate conversations when other people are dull.
Or, again, there are those days when you don't want to
see people at all but would like just to stay home and
work in the garden. Thinking of the psychotic as "withdrawn," I suppose, you wish not to be like him.

Let's look at it another way. If you examine your daily
life cycle, you will find you are withdrawn for approxi-
mately eight hours in sleep, are more-or-less involved with
other people at work for about eight hours, after which
there are eight hours of relationships with family and
friends. About half our existence, then involves people.
It would be unnatural to want a great deal more. No
matter how self-actualizing you may be, you must get
away at times.

Although manipulation usually involves withdrawal
from contactful expression, one can be manipulative by
maintaining a relationship beyond its nourishing value.
A manipulator is described by Perls as a "Clinger" or
"Hanging-on Biter." [2] The Clinger is the one who won't
give up, but keeps right on talking to you, though he
realizes the conversation is finished. This is not a matter
of social awkwardness, of not knowing how to terminate
the exchange, but a neurotic fear on the part of this individual that he hasn't said all he wants to say. He's so
insecure he can't let go. This fear costs people jobs when
they go for interviews and having said something once,

they keep trying to say it again and invariably louse it all up. The Hanging-on Biter is that other recognizable individual who hangs on to a conversation like a bulldog with a stick. He isn't aware he has outlived the usefulness of the contact. Rather than bite it off, he braces himself like a bulldog and stands there vigorously shaking the conversational stick.

Withdrawal may be characterized either as manipulative or actualizing. Healthy withdrawal is the ability temporarily to abandon contact with another person or situation when it is no longer productive or when the contact becomes painful. A healthy, actualizing withdrawal is *toward* something (I am tired and must break this off because my organism needs rest), but essentially it is toward a position of self-respect. The manipulative withdrawal, on the other hand, is to isolate oneself permanently or escape from contact with others. For instance, you are afraid to talk with someone because you might be embarrassed, or someone is angry, so you avoid them.

Contact Through Emotions

For contact to be understood quite clearly, let me place it in a theoretical frame of reference. Excitement is the basic life energy of the individual. It seeks to express itself in contact with other human beings. *Emotions are the means by which we make contact.* We may talk angrily or warmly toward another; both are good contact or potential contact, for contact is established only if it has the support of our emotions.

Control Through Partially Blocked Emotions

The manipulator, failing to express the basic contact emotions—anger, fear, hurt, trust, and love—resorts to

67

other blocked or partial emotions. Worrying and sadness are two. Sadness will last indefinitely if it isn't given expression in deep hurt or crying. Worrying is like nibbling on food. The worrier doesn't take full action but represses aggression, and passivity results.

Resentment is another incomplete emotion. It is, in truth, incomplete and unorganismically and unopenly expressed anger. Any unexpressed emotions, turned inward, result in feelings of resignation and depression.

Embarrassment is defined as the tendency to make contact and hide from contact at the same time. For reasons that should be obvious, Perls calls the emotions of embarrassment and shame "Quisling emotions." [3] Like the Norwegian who assisted the Nazis against his own countrymen, these emotions obstruct and arrest their own organism, rather than assist it. As Quislings, they identify with the enemy. They are blocked by repression and therefore are most painful to reexpress.

Awareness of blocked or partial emotions and the ability to endure them is a prime requisite for actualization. If these blocked emotions can be endured, they tend to reactualize into the basic feelings of fear, hurt, anger, trust, and love. The actualizor isn't reluctant to show shame or embarrassment because he understands they are very human feelings. His goal is to be able to show them honestly.

NOTES

1. Jay Haley, *Strategies of Psychotherapy* (New York: Grune & Stratton, 1963), pp. 89-90.

2. Frederick Perls, *Ego, Hunger and Aggression* (London: George Allen and Unwin, 1947), p. 108.

3. *Ibid.*, p. 178.

CHAPTER 5
Honestly Being Your Feelings

"Now don't be upset. . . . Control yourself. . . . Take it easy," constantly cautions the manipulator.

Well he might since this is a big part of his problem. He is a person who can't allow you to get angry at him and must always prevent you from confronting him with the impact of your ideas.

A major defense against manipulation, therefore, would

be for the rest of us to learn to become *honestly* expressive with our own feelings.

The Nature of Feelings

The truth is that most of us do not understand, although we live with them every day of our lives, what it means to *experience* our feelings, either physiologically or consciously. Some of us don't even know what they are. The result is we never learn to *communicate* them accurately or clearly and sentence ourselves to life in a constant Tower of Babel. It will be good here to take a look at those five basic contact emotions.

1. *Anger.* What is the physiological message you receive when you feel angry? What is your body telling you? How do you know you are angry? You want to fight, that's what. (Fighting, of course, may only be verbal.) How do you know you want to fight? Your whole system says so. You breathe faster, and your heart beats faster; your muscles begin to contract, and you get tense and actually have a sensation of heat. Most people, at least, experience a hot, flushed feeling when angry. Whether it be a verbal or physical fight, or just little acts of angry behavior, our bodies must do *something* when we are angry, and the worst thing we can do is to repress them.

2. *Fear.* How do you know when your body is fearful? The feeling is almost the opposite of anger. Your mouth gets dry, you feel cold, your palms begin to sweat. Shake hands with someone who is frightened, and you usually will feel the cold sweat.

3. *Hurt.* Most of us seem basically afraid to be hurt, and I suspect it's because of many manipulators in our lives who caution us not to hurt *their* feelings. They trap us

easily when we aren't aware of their game. "Why don't you do something about that?" someone asks, and we reply almost automatically: "Well, I wouldn't want to hurt anyone." Why not, if to do what needs doing is right? For instance, what if you notice that your neighbors' fourteen-year-old is sneaking their car out in their absence and might, with his obvious want of driving skills, cause a fatal accident?

An unreasonable shrinking of one's own world to keep from hurting anybody or anything is, of course, a symptom of neurosis. Obviously, it is most important for us to know when we are doing it. It isn't only that we are afraid of hurting others, either, but we're afraid that they are going to hurt us. Maybe the neighbor will tell us our own son is sneaking out with our car. Maybe they'll just tell us to mind our own business. That could hurt our pride.

Hurting is a very difficult feeling for the average individual to express. When you actually are *feeling* hurt, you are withdrawn and regressive, as if you wanted to go back into your mother's womb. One of the symptoms we all recognize is crying. Women, for many reasons, are not at all afraid to show feelings this way; but men in our culture never are supposed to. Back in childhood, no doubt, someone has manipulated them out of their tears by cautioning: "Now, now, Johnny, big boys don't cry." Tillich says most of us don't have "the courage of despair" —we're actually afraid to feel bad. Yet this unexpressed hurt can be an overpowering noose about the neck of an individual. I remember all too poignantly the desperate look in the eyes of a man who blurted: "I wish more than anything on this earth that I could have a real 24-carat feeling of being hurt." No thanks to the manipulative habits of a lifetime, could he have that feeling and the great relief of melting into natural, human tears.

4. *Trust*. This fourth fundamental feeling is experienced in a feeling of openness. When you trust someone, you are saying: "Here I am, I trust you, now it's up to you." The opposite is, of course, distrust, a feeling of not being free, not being able to be yourself with another.

5. Finally there is *love*. Love is the golden key to the creative use of all the other feelings; yet how little we know of it! Shelley called it "poets' food"; Goldsmith "an abject intercourse between tyrants and slaves." I like the definition of Rainer Maria Rilke, the German poet: "Love consists in this, that two solitudes protect and touch and greet each other."

From a psychological standpoint it is vital to know when your body is feeling a sense of love, and I commend to you Erich Fromm's *The Art of Loving*. It is one of the most fundamental books ever written on love, which he calls "the active concern for life and the growth of that which we love." [1] Again, our body will tell us physiologically when we are feeling lovable or loving. Think of love as a warm-glow emotion and anger as a hot emotion.

Still it is an interesting fact that the two feelings are very close. How often we find we get angrily hot before we can get lovingly warm. To express love, we have to take the risk of first expressing the four other feelings, and certainly this has important implications in human relationships, particularly marriage. A person can never have a true and lasting relationship with another until he is able to fight with him. When we're able to show we *are* angry, that we *are* afraid, that we *can* be hurt and *can* trust—then we can love. When we can really level with each other, telling each other how we feel and getting all our feelings out in the open, only then do we begin to feel this closeness. Love, by this set of standards, is obviously a fulfillment of all other feelings.

Therapists prefer to have both marriage partners in for therapy because if only one learns to express his feelings and the other does not, it could hurt the marriage more. Two manipulators may get along together tolerably, but if one begins actualizing, then there is real trouble. Two actualizers will not make a "happy" marriage necessarily, but it will be challenging, exciting, and conflictual. They will cope with each other rather than avoiding each other or being falsely and hypocritically "sweet." As a matter of fact, being actualizers, they will enjoy the conflict rather than avoid it.

Manipulating the Feelings of Others

When each of the five fundamental feelings are expressed honestly, then the individual is beginning to actualize. On the other hand, we know that the manipulator is aware of the importance of these feelings as well and will often try to use them to control other people. The following are some examples:

1. *Anger.* A manipulator can, by his own anger, intimidate and create fear in others. For example, we all have met manipulators who, by their shouting and screaming, keep other people from communicating with them. Other clever manipulators use the feeling of anger by getting people to hate.

2. *Fear.* Eugene Burdick suggests that a manipulator works fear along with hate. "He sits at the console and gives 'em what he thinks they need; a little fear today,

a little hate tomorrow. Some days he gives 'em both. And they stand together and shiver and think he's the greatest guy in the world and love him." [2]

3. *Hurt.* The author of *How to Be a Jewish Mother* gives examples of how a manipulative mother might use hurt to control her children. He calls it the "Technique of Basic Suffering":

To master the Technique of Basic Suffering you should begin with an intensive study of the Dristan commercials on television. Pay particular attention to the face of the actor who has not yet taken Dristan.

Note the squint of the eyes, the furrow of the brow, the downward curve of the lips—the pained expression which can only come from eight undrained sinus cavities or severe gastritis.

The following key phrases illustrate the use of hurt to control:
   a. "Go ahead and enjoy yourself" (and don't worry that I have a headache).
   b. "Don't worry about me."
   c. "I don't mind staying home alone."
   d. "I'm glad it happened to me and not to you." [3]

4. *Trust.* The typical "con artist" uses trust to make a sale. The word "con" comes from the word confidence, and this supersalesman tries to instill confidence and trust in himself by various methods. He gets you to believe that his company is the most reputable in the world, his product is the finest there is, and that he is the most honest man in the world. Finally, when he gets you to sign for his product, he says, "Remember now, I'll trust you to pay C.O.D. for this when it arrives."

5. *Love.* The use of love as a manipulative technique is illustrated by such phrases as "If you love me you would. . . ." Many a young widow has experienced a greedy man asking to participate in her fortune by getting her to fall in love with him. The use of love as a manipulation is a common one. Dan Greenberg gives the following seven basic sacrifices ironically, of course, by which a mother might manipulate a son by love:

a. Stay up all night to prepare him a big breakfast.
b. Go without lunch so you can put an extra apple in his lunchpail.
c. Give up an evening of work with a charitable institution so that he can have the car on a date.
d. Tolerate the girl he's dating.
e. Don't let him know you fainted twice in the supermarket from fatigue. (But make sure he knows you're not letting him know.)
f. When he comes home from the dentist, take over his toothache for him.
g. Open his bedroom window wider so he can have more fresh air, and close your own so you don't use up the supply.[4]

Counterfeit Patterns of the Manipulator

Before we can achieve the creative awareness that we need to overcome the manipulations in our lives, we have to learn to identify, experience, and honestly express the real feelings we have. The manipulator develops instead a whole repertoire of counterfeit patterns for his everyday life. You will recognize the common ones.

1. *Substituting one emotion for another.* Many of us express anger when it's really hurt we feel. We do this because anger is a more predictable emotion. We know

what will happen when we are angry—the other party will get angry too, and we are ready for that. When we are hurt, however, we have to open up ourselves to the other person, and we don't know what might happen. So, since we're afraid to trust them, we show anger instead, substituting one emotion for the other. Thus, we see the lady, tears welling in her eyes, cry out: "You make me mad!" She isn't mad at all; she's hurt. Another time, using the same counterfeit manipulative pattern, we express anger when we're actually afraid. Here we have the backseat driver growling: "Stop driving so fast or you'll get arrested." What he means is: "When you drive so fast, I'm scared."

Don't think for a moment that all of us don't, at times, resort to this pattern of substituting. We say to a grieving friend: "I feel as bad as you about this." We are nearing an expression of love here, but we aren't really loving. Love would be expressed by the simple statement: "I care for you, I care about this, and I grieve." To say this, though, entails taking a risk, and too often we are afraid to. We may release our tears when someone else is hurting in the hope it will show our love, but it doesn't. We have to say it, clearly and distinctly: "I love you."

2. *Getting on the emotional merry-go-round.* Here we feel so many feelings at one time that we don't express any of them adequately enough to communicate to the other person. Instead, we offer only confusion. A woman in hysterics does this; one feeling after another pops to the surface, but none stays long enough to develop fully. She is manipulating because, by expressing all these feelings in a confused outburst, she does not allow any response. Thus she can control those about her to get what she wants.

For example, Mother doesn't want to go off for a family weekend, as Dad has planned; so she gets sick. The family shows its disappointment, and now she climbs on the emotional merry-go-round. She jumps from being mad at Dad to expressions of fear for the children's health should they go without her, to not trusting the veterinarian to care for their dog, although he has done it many times. After thoroughly confusing everyone, she resorts to sulking to get her way and stays at home.

3. *Feeling our feelings only as a delayed reaction.* Here we meet the person whose pace is so slow he says: "I was mad at you last week." *Last week?* It took him a week to find it out? Not really. He knew how he felt last week but in the workings of the manipulative mind rationalized: If you don't know I am mad at you now, we won't make contact. That contact is what he must avoid. I have seen this in therapy when a patient opens a meeting by declaring: "I was mad last week about Jane and her talk of abortion." What this devious remark means is: I know it's old enough now that I won't be attacked by you for saying it.

4. *Making a virtue of not being aware that one has any normal feelings.* Most of us know the man who boasts: "My wife and I have a wonderful marriage—we never fight." To such a declaration I am apt to explode: "Tommyrot!" Just being normal, people are like sandpaper and must rub each other the wrong way at times. Of course they have fights. They have them because they have feelings, normal feelings, as much as they would like to appear virtuously free of them.

5. *Confusing our feelings with facts.* You say to someone: "You're stupid!" It isn't a fact at all since you haven't

actually measured their intelligence. Nevertheless, many of us suffer from the misconception that an opinion, if it comes from within us, is really a fact. If you said instead, "I *feel* you are stupid," then you might well be stating the fact. (And you might also provoke a punch in the nose.)

6. *Feeling "with one's hand on the doorknob."* Such a person may let true feelings slip out but is ready to run the instant anyone reacts to him. Afraid of people's reactions to his feelings, he runs from them.

We read in I Corinthians, "When I was a child, I spake as a child, I understood as a child, I thought as a child: but when I became a man, I put away childish things." The difficulty with manipulators is that though they become adults and speak as adults and think as adults, they continue to *feel* as children. They avoid any tendencies toward self-actualization, which is the process of learning to do business with our emotions. For one thing, there are no short cuts to this knowledge. To achieve even a vestige of it, we must go back and relearn the fundamental emotions.

Congruence and Actualization

A key to opening the doors of dealing with our feelings is what Carl Rogers calls "congruence." By congruence we mean being able to feel our feelings physiologically, to communicate them accurately, and to experience them consciously. If we can do all three, there is congruence between the unconscious, conscious, and communication process, and we *feel* as though we are actualizing.

The manipulator is *not* congruent. When his conscious communication is out of phase with feelings felt only viscerally, he is said to be *deceitful.* For example, when we tell the hostess we have had a good time at her party when actually we were bored stiff, we are not expressing what we feel internally. Being perfectly honest, but still polite, we might say: "Thank you for inviting us." (And can't you imagine what will happen across America if hostesses suddenly find all their departing guests saying politely: "Thank you—.") When the manipulator's conscious awareness is out of phase with his physiological awareness, he is said to be *defensive*. Example: A person's expressing anger behaviorally while denying it verbally. "Are you angry?" his friend asks. I have been clenching my fist, and now I slam the table and shout: "No! I am NOT angry!" My body is angry, as any fool can plainly see, but I refuse to admit it. Rarely are the manipulator's words in tune with his body.

Manipulative Communication Patterns

Our greatest problem with our feelings comes in communication. There are two elements to communication, sending and receiving. Like radio transmitters, we are sending out messages constantly. The problem is whether the people about us are getting the messages we send. We all have the problem of trying to make someone understand exactly what we say or feel. Consider some of the problems manipulators have in this area of communications.

The first involves errors in *sending,* and one of these is the *unexpressed expectation.* It's Mother's Day, let's say, and Mom secretly has hoped someone will offer breakfast in bed or that there will be a nice gift with breakfast. She *hopes* one of these things will happen but hasn't mentioned it to anyone, least of all Dad. Nothing happens.

Here's a sending error, an unexpressed expectation, and Mom is disappointed. In marriage and other close human relationships, we have hosts of such expectations and never take the time, or are afraid, really to *ask for the things we want.*

The actualizor knows this, for he knows quite a bit about communications. He doesn't want to go through life misunderstood. He knows, therefore, that many misunderstandings can be avoided if only he declares, or asks for, what he wants. A good part of the feeling of not being understood, for most of us, can be traced directly to the fact that we do not really communicate our needs. If we want something, then we ought to be able to ask for it, no matter what it may be.

A second type of sending error is what we call the *contrived expectation.* Here we manipulate the other person's response by the way we state our expectation. "You didn't get in until two A.M." you say to your spouse. It probably was much earlier, as you know, but by making it worse you expect him to reply: "No, it was only one." Many of us manipulate by anticipating the worst in the hope of getting something better.

The other major communication problem is in *receiving,* and here we make just as many errors as we do in sending. For instance, we may appear to *ignore a message* which we really aren't ignoring at all. Someone says something that hurts us quite badly, but we won't say, "That hurts." Ignoring it, we simply don't respond at all and then begin to feel crushed.

Another receiving error is to *neutralize the communication* sent us. Here may be a measure of one's ability to receive love. Someone says: "You look very lovely tonight."

Rather than replying, "Thank you very much, I appreciate the compliment," we respond: "Oh, you look lovely, too." It's almost as if we are afraid to feel good when someone gives us this feeling. We keep throwing it back so that we don't have to feel the impact of the sent feeling. I run into this situation frequently in therapy, and I tell people: "You're just gypping yourself, canceling out a gift of love. When anyone tells you you look good, it's like money in the bank. Accept it gladly."

A third receiving error is always to *respond in terms of the other person's expectations*. No matter what they say, we give back what they want, even though we don't feel it at all. "Do you like my new suit?" coaxes a friend, and you reply dutifully: "Oh, I think it looks great." The truth may be that you wonder how he could have bought such a turkey. You might reply, "Well, I like the cut of the jacket," or even, "No, I can't say I do." There's nothing wrong with disagreeing on clothing, except that in this country we labor under a Dale Carnegie complex and believe we must always be winning friends and influencing people.

Finally, we may *respond as if the other person's message is contrived:* What is it she really wants to know? I have to figure out how to respond so I don't give her what she wants. We see this in marriage when the wife asks at dinner: "How *did* you like the roast beef?" Her manipulating husband happens to be one of those individuals who believes that half of what his spouse says is contrived, and he's just not going to give her the reply she wants. One rule of his game is never to allow her to get satisfaction from her cooking. So he replies: "Frankly, it's not as good as my mother used to cook," or, "Well, it's the best roast beef I've had today."

Actualizing Communication Patterns

Actualization, on the other hand, is the ability to send and receive communications honestly. It means giving up all the manipulative patterns we have discussed so far in this chapter. It means frequently we first must risk ourselves whenever we send out a feeling. The existentialists make much of this these days. They contend that you really have to put yourself on the line with your feelings. Nevertheless, in their system you have no expectations; you let the emotional chips fall where they may.

Actualized sending naturally involves *honest* sending, and the messages sent must be responded to honestly. Here we find one of the greatest differences between the introvert and extrovert. Many extroverts can send out messages fairly directly and openly and also can receive them very quickly and make a response. Others of us, more on the introverted side, have to take a little time before we really know what our response is. We all need to respect the fact that people have different speeds or paces of feelings and it takes more time for some than it does for others to react honestly.

If you are one who tends always to give what is wanted rather than what you really feel, there are three steps you can take: *delay, become aware* of what internal response seems best, then *react*. While computing, stay with the subject; don't flit on to something else. Your reaction will always come. Your neighbor says she doesn't like your coffee cake? Delay a moment and compute the inner response. You do have a reacting mechanism. See what it says; then respond. It may take a little time, and you won't always react perfectly, but you will see what seeming miracles come with practice.

It is a solid principle of actualization that a healthy relationship does not always have to be an agreeing relationship. Some of our best marriages and departmental relations come from the fact that people have entirely different points of view and feelings about things and that we respect their differences. We do not have to agree. Too often in life there are problems about which we make the unconscious assumption that in order to have harmony we must also have agreement.

An actualizor who honestly feels is particularly aware of the danger of the indifference manipulation. He *never pretends* to have given up, to be indifferent to, not to care for those he honestly cares about. He avoids such stock phrases as "I give up," "You're hopeless," "I've had it," etc. Instead, he tells honestly of his gripes, wants, and hopes, believing in directness of communication as the means whereby love is best maintained.

Basically, the actualizing relationship is an active caring. A person's ability to go deeply into himself is determined by the other person's ability to do the same. As a relationship develops, we must be accepting and permissive, but we must also be able to react with our own feelings of discouragement, anger, or whatever feeling we have.

NOTES

1. Erich Fromm, *The Art of Loving* (Colophon ed.; New York: Harper & Row, [1956] 1962), p. 26.
2. Eugene Burdick, *The Ninth Wave* (Boston: Houghton Mifflin Company, 1956), p. 90.
3. Dan Greenburg, *How to Be a Jewish Mother* (Los Angeles: Price/Stern/Sloan Publishers, 1965), pp. 15, 16.
4. *Ibid.,* p. 17.

CHAPTER 6

Trusting Yourself in the Here and Now

I would like to give special attention to the matter of time and its relationship to manipulation and actualization.

A significant variable which sets the manipulator apart from the actualizing person is his approach to time. For one, it's the past which provides excuses for his failures; for another, the future on which he can base his promises. The present-oriented manipulator is the busybody who never accomplishes much but talks a lot about it.

The Present vs. Past and Future

In my Personal Orientation Inventory [1], I have formulated items related to the time dimension and believe the following conclusions to be warranted:

1. The manipulator who is past-oriented is characterized by guilt, regret, remorse, blaming, and resentments. He is a person who still is nibbling on the undigested memories of the past. He is the depressive who keeps nibbling at past hurts. For instance,

> I feel so bad about what happened to Father that life has no meaning for me now.

> I feel so guilty that I didn't take better care of the house and children. Now I have nothing.

> If my parents only encouraged me to go to school, I'd be interested now. It's their fault I can't get started.

> I resent that teacher. How do you expect me to do any good work for him?

2. The manipulator who is future-oriented is an individual who lives continually in terms of idealized goals, plans, expectations, predictions, and fears. He is the obsessive worrier who nibbles at the future.

> Someday I'll get going and return to school. I've got too many responsibilities now.

> Next summer I plan to get the yard work done.

> You wait and see—I'll be working here long after those guys are gone.

> I'm so worried about what is going to happen I just can't do anything right now.

> I promise to do better next time.

85

3. The pathological manipulator who is present-oriented is the individual whose past does not contribute to the present in a meaningful way and who has no future goals tied to present activity. He is a person who engages in meaningless activity and unreflective concentration—the busybody who is always actively avoiding facing himself. He would say:

> I've got so many responsibilities right now I just don't have time to think.

> I have three children and a husband to care for, and I don't have time to think of myself.

> Please love me—I've got so much on my mind.

> I've made a list of all the things I'm doing today.

4. The actualizing person, by POI measurements, is an individual who is primarily time competent. He is concerned with living fully in the present though he uses the past and future to make the present more meaningful. He understands that memory and anticipation are *acts in the present*. The focus, therefore, is on the present, with past and future as background.

On page 87 is a well-known textbook example of the figure-ground phenomenon. A white chalice on a black background or if the white area is taken as ground, then the figure becomes two heads in profile silhouette. As one continues to study this ambiguous picture, he can switch from one way of looking at it to the other but never can look at it both ways at once. If the chalice in the center becomes the primary focus, however, representing the present, the faces of the past and future become meaningly related as background to the chalice. This symbolizes the way the actualizing person relates the three dimensions of time.

> "I am working on my term paper this weekend. I've been collecting materials since the beginning of the semester. I'll have it done by the deadline in three weeks."

> "I will finish my work for the Associate of Arts degree this semester. I've learned that if I do just a few units every semester, I'll get through. I plan eventually to get my B.A."

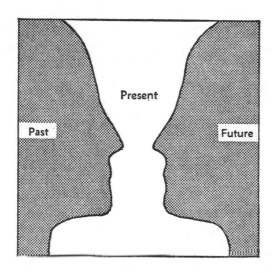

Inner vs. Other-Direction

To understand actualization, one needs first to appreciate the concepts of other-direction, inner-direction.[2]

The inner-directed person, as I interpret it, appears to incorporate early in life a psychic gyroscope that is set going by parental influences, later to be influenced further by other authority figures. The inner-directed man goes through life apparently independent but still obeying this internal piloting. The source of his inner direction is implanted early, and it is guided by a small number of principles. Although the source of direction for the individual is inner, in that it is implanted early in life, it later becomes generalized as an inner core of principles and character traits. A danger of excessive inner-directness is that the individual might become insensitive to the rights and feelings of others and could feel that he can manipulate them authoritatively because of his own inner sense of "rightness." Examples:

"My feelings can be trusted."

"Whatever I decide, I must make my own decision."

"What I want is what I do."

The other-directed person, because of insecurity and doubt on the part of his parents of how to bring him up, has been motivated to develop a radar system to receive signals from a far wider circle than just his parents. The boundaries between familial authority and other external authorities break down, and his primary feeling tends to be *fear* of the fluctuating voices of "authorities" or his peer group. The danger of other-directedness is that manipulation, in the form of pleasing others and insuring constant acceptance, becomes his primary method of relating. Thus it may be seen that the original feeling of fear can be transformed into an obsessive, insatiable need for affection or reassurance of being loved. Examples:

"What will people think?"

"Tell me what you think I should do."

"What is the right thing to do?"

The self-actualizing person tends to be less dependency-
or deficiency-oriented than either the extreme inner- or
the extreme other-directed person. He may be characterized as having more of an autonomous, self-supportive, or
being orientation. He is other-directed in that he must
to a degree be sensitive to people's approval, affection,
and good will; but the source of his actions is essentially
inner-directed. He is more inner-directed although his
freedom is not gained by being a rebel or by pushing
against others and fighting them. He transcends complete
inner-directedness by critical assimilation and creative
expansion of his earlier principles of living. He has discovered an inner mode of living which gives him confidence. Examples:

"I check with those who love me and then make my
own decisions."

"I gather as much data as possible on the problems and
consequences and then trust my deepest feelings for
the decision."

"I am free from their pressure, but I still am interested
in what they think."

Relation Between Present Orientation and Actualization

Our research shows that there is a parallel or correla-
tion between actualization and time competence.[3] The
reason probably lies in the fact that a self-actualizing person, *living in the present, trusts more his own self-support*
and his own self-expressiveness than does the person who
lives more in the past or future. In other words, one can-

not depend on anything *but* freely experiencing life and himself when he lives in a here-and-now orientation to life.

"I have tried to express this," says Maslow, "as a contrast between *living fully* and *preparing* to live fully, between *growing up* and *being grown.*" [4]

The person who lives in the future relies on expected events to motivate him. Frederick Perls suggests that ideals or goals are means by which the need for affection, appreciation, and admiration is being gratified. A person gratifies his vanity by picturing himself in terms of his goals. These invented goals are developed because he is incapable of accepting himself as he is in the here-and-now since he lost awareness of his biological being in the here-and-now. He invents a meaning for life to justify his experience. By striving for the goal of future perfection, he turns his own life into a living hell. He achieves just the opposite of his intentions with this idealistic attitude, arrests his own development, and promotes inferiority feelings in himself.

By the same token, the individual who lives in the past relies on blaming others as a substitute for self-support. Our problems exist in the here-and-now, regardless of when they were born, and their solutions must be found in the here-and-now. Quite literally, the only time we possibly can live in is the present. We can *remember* the past; we can *anticipate* the future, but we *live* only in the present. Even when we reexperience the past, we have not reversed time. We have, in effect, only moved the past up to the present. So if psychotherapy is to help us solve our problems, it must work within the only framework we have, the here-and-now.

Conclusions

It is important to stress again that memory (*from the past*) and anticipation (*toward the future*) are acts in the *present*. "Now here I am *remembering* my mistakes," says the patient, and note the difference between that and merely wandering off into memory. Or he might say: "I am *planning* (expecting) to do the job on Wednesday," and we would have to consider it as more than idle anticipation.

The manipulator given to reminiscence of the past or idle talk of the future is not refreshed by these mental wanderings. Actually, he is exhausted and empty; such behavior is not active, but passive. As Perls implies, one's worthiness cannot be given in explanations for the past nor by promises for the future. "It wasn't my fault," whines the manipulator in referring to the past. "I'm as good as anybody else." Referring to the future, he says: "I'm not very well right now, but I'll make my mark." The actualizor, unlike either of these, gets his feeling of worthiness from his adequacy in an *activity* that is going on or in relaxation after a completed situation. Explaining or promising is felt by him to be a lie, either consoling or self-punishing. But to *do* something and *be* oneself is self-trusting and self-justifying. Examples of self-actualizing present behavior:

"I feel so good, so alive, working in the yard today."

"Gee it's fun just running, jumping, and being free."

"I feel like a good sleep—I've really got a lot done today."

"I feel like a duck swimming on top of the water. I'm really doing what I am capable of, fully!"

91

Looking closer at this idea of the healthy individual as being the one who lives primarily in the present, we see that *living fully* in the moment or the present requires no concern for support or sustenance. To say "I *am* adequate now," rather than "I *was* adequate once," or "I will be adequate again," is self-validating and self-justifying. Being—in the moment, being—an active process, is an end in itself. It is self-validating and self-justifying. *Being has its own reward—a feeling of trust in one's self-support.*

Maslow says a person experiencing time in this way is one living in a state of "creative innocence."

In the child there is a total unquestioning acceptance of whatever happens. Since there is also very little memory, *very little leaning on the past,* there is little tendency in the child to bring the past into the present or into the future. The consequence is that the child is totally without past and future.

If one expects nothing, if one has no anticipations or apprehensions, if in a certain sense *there is no future,* because the child is moving totally "here—now," there can be no surprise, no disappointment. One thing is as likely as another to happen. This is "perfect waiting" and spectatorship without any demands that one thing happen rather than another. There is no prognosis. And no prediction means no worry, no anxiety, no apprehension or foreboding.

This is all related to my conception of the creative personality as one who is totally here—now, *one who lives without future or past.* Another way of saying this is: "The creative person is an innocent." An innocent could be defined as a grown person who can still perceive, or think, or react like a child. It is this innocence that is recovered in the "second naïveté, or perhaps I will call it the "second innocence" of the wise old man who has managed to recover the ability to be childlike.[5]

The poet Kahlil Gibran has expressed it this way:

> The timeless in you is aware of life's timeliness.
> And knows that yesterday is but today's memory
> and tomorrow is today's dream.
>
> .   .   .   .
>
> And let today embrace the past with remembrance
> and the future with longing.[6]

Summary

The manipulator may be past-oriented and using his past as excuses for failure, or he may be future-oriented and using the future for promises which never materialize. He can also be the present-oriented person who *talks* about everything he is doing but gets none of it done. He spends most of his time justifying and defending himself. If he is passive, he is a cryer, a blamer asking for love in spite of his bad luck. If he is active, he cons us into believing he has achieved when he hasn't really. Both forms of manipulation give pseudo-support and justification in that the deception of another person gives him a feeling of power. If he were deeply honest, he would have to admit that his con ventures are empty and unfulfilling.

The actualizor, on the other hand (as always), is a doer, a *be*-er. He achieves expression in his own feelings and talents in an effort to cope generally with life in the present. He feels good about himself because his existence is filled with ongoing activity. He experiences self-support and self-expression in freely living life in the here and now. He moves freely back and forth into the past for memories and into the future for goals but remembers that these, too, are acts of the present from which self-support comes.

For the actualizor, life is an exciting process of trusting himself in the here and now.

NOTES

1. E. L. Shostrom, *Personal Orientation Inventory* (San Diego: Educational and Industrial Testing Service, 1964).

2. These terms have been adapted from David Riesman, *The Lonely Crowd* (Garden City, N. Y.: Doubleday Anchor Books, 1950).

3. "A Test for the Measurement of Self-Actualization," *Educational and Psychological Measurement,* XXIV (1965), 207-18.

4. Abraham H. Maslow, *Toward a Psychology of Being* (Princeton, N. J.: D. Van Nostrand & Co., 1962), p. 30.

5. Abraham H. Maslow, "Innocent Cognition (as an aspect of B-Cognition)," *Notes on B-Psychology* (La Jolla, Calif.: Western Behavior Sciences Institute, August 31, 1961). pp. 1-2.

6. Kahlil Gibran, *The Prophet* (New York: Alfred A. Knopf, 1923), pp. 70-71. Used by permission.

CHAPTER 7

Freedom and Awareness

Having examined the honest use of feelings in which *honesty* of expression was posited as a prime requirement for actualization, and having seen that the actualizor has a deep *trust* in himself and others to cope with life in the here and now, we come now to the final two characteristics of actualization—*freedom* and *awareness.*

Freedom

The process of understanding man is a complex one, and it has been a measure of the greatness of writers down through the ages that they have given us some understanding. Among the writings of one of the ablest, we find this cogent paragraph:

One of the most widespread superstitions is that every man has his own special, definite qualities; that a man is kind, cruel, wise, stupid, energetic, apathetic, etc. Men are not like that ... men are like rivers: the water is the same in each, and alike in all; but every river is narrow here, is more rapid there, here slower, there broader, now clear, now cold, now dull, now warm. It is the same with men. Every man carries in himself the germs of every human quality, and sometimes one manifests itself, sometimes another, and the man often becomes unlike himself, while still remaining the same man.[1]

We have suggested, for purposes of exposition, that man comes in two broad categories, the manipulator and the actualizor, and yet, as Tolstoy says, man has within himself the potential for every human quality. Each man is a manipulator, as we have seen, but he is also an actualizor. The important fact seems to be that he has a continuing choice—freedom to choose one or the other. By freedom we do not mean simply freedom *from* the control of others, but rather freedom *to actualize*. Freedom is the choice and responsibility taken for a style of expression we use.[2] Erich Fromm believes that man "has the freedom to create, to construct, to wonder, to venture." He goes on to define freedom as the capacity to make a choice, to choose between alternatives.[3] Only when we are aware of our manipulations are we free to experience them and to derive from them actualizing behavior. The actualizor is free to be master of his life; he is a subject and not a puppet or an object.

The actualizor is free in the sense that, while he may play the game of life, he is *aware* he is playing it. He plays it "tongue in cheek," Alan Watts says. He realizes that he manipulates sometimes and is manipulated at other times. *But he is aware of the manipulation.* He does not try to change the manipulator lest at that moment he becomes himself a manipulator. Taking the responsibility to change another is, you see, only to be manipulated by that person. One may *describe* him or *confront* him with his manipulation, but one need not take responsibility to change him. The actualizor recognizes that each person must ultimately take that responsibility for himself.

The actualizor is aware that life need not be a serious game at all, but rather is more akin to a dance. No one wins or loses in a dance; a dance is a process. The actualizor dances or skates between all his complimentary potentials. What is important is enjoying the *process* of living rather than achieving the *ends* of living. Since actualizing people appreciate the doing itself, for its own sake, they enjoy the process of getting someplace as much as the arriving. One psychologist believes it is possible for them to make an intrinsically enjoyable game or dance or play out of the most trivial and routine activity.[4] The actualizor swings with life and does not take it with dead seriousness. The manipulator, on the other hand, sees life as a rat race and takes it so seriously he is frequently the candidate for a nervous breakdown.

Surrender or Nonstriving

As Abraham Maslow has pointed out, our Western culture rests generally on Judaic-Christian theology, and the United States is dominated particularly by a puritan spirit which stresses activity, striving, and hard work.[5] Karen Horney speaks of the Apollonian and Dionysian tendencies, the latter stressing the value of surrender and drift, the former emphasizing the mastery and molding of life. Both are natural human tendencies, she says, and the positive value of surrender or nonstriving is a deep-rooted human attitude which is pregnant with potential satisfaction.[6]

Nonstriving or "Letting Be" has been defined by James Bugental as the "willing assent to the is-ness of awareness without striving and without effortful concentration and decision-making."[7] He regards nonstriving as an important characteristic of the actualizing life.

In *The Power of Sexual Surrender,* Robinson also stresses the importance of surrender in her discussion of sexual relationship.[8] She describes surrender and passivity as a natural feminine function, which many masculinized women of today have lost. She further sees modern women as trying to be responsible for everything and competing with men. In sexual intercourse and in life, she says, man is active and women more passive. This writer would suggest that both men and women have passive potentials, but women have lost the power of their passive potential— perhaps more than men. To have faith in another person means to be able to surrender to that person, and active intercourse is a synergistic process of giving and receiving, of mastery and surrender, synergistically being both one's active and passive potentials at the same time. Alan Watts puts the value of nonstriving in another context:

I have always been fascinated by the law of reversed effort. Sometimes I call it the "backwards law." When you try to stay on the surface of the water, you sink; but when you try to sink you float. When you hold your breath you lose it—which immediately calls to mind an ancient and most neglected saying, "Whosoever would save his soul shall lose it." Insecurity is the result of trying to be secure, and that, contrariwise, salvation and sanity consist in the most radical recognition that we have no way of saving ourselves. The Chinese sage Lao-tzu, that master of the law of reversed effort . . . declared that those who justify themselves do not convince, that to know truth one must get rid of knowledge, and that nothing is more powerful and creative than emptiness—from which men shrink.[9]

What Watts is saying is that the more we *try* in some situations, the more we seem to fail, and there are some goals which can never be achieved by active striving. We find this particularly true in psychotherapy when the more one tries to become a certain way, the more one fails.

Leslie H. Farber speaks of the paradoxical nature of certain qualities of being and the impossibility of striving for such qualities as wisdom, dignity, courage, humility. The thing that characterizes each of these virtues is that one's possession of them lies outside of conscious effort.

Most accomplishments and some virtues do not have this *paradoxical* nature. Skill or tact or a capacity for honesty, for example, may be pursued directly; to acknowledge and enjoy possession of them does not contradict their nature. But only the fool proclaims his wisdom, only the proud man his humility, only the coward his courage. Not only do these virtues make a liar of the man who claims them, they forever evade any effort to achieve them. I may seek knowledge; I may not seek to be wise. Sharing an essential freedom from self-concern . . . such virtues are not accomplishments and cannot be learned. They must be deserved, but their possession is a matter of grace.[10]

Understanding this is extremely important in self-actualization, for it means that the most profound qualities of actualization, such as wisdom, dignity, humility, courage, respect, and love *cannot be striven for!* They cannot be learned and are most often achieved when one surrenders to the impossibility of being them. In psychotherapy, for example, we hear a patient striving to be "real"; the more he strives, the phonier he becomes. After many hours, he finally says, "Oh nuts! I give up. I just can't seem to make it." In that moment, paradoxically, he is real! The religious patient is another. The more he strives to be humble, the more he becomes proud. Curiously, the most lovable person is one who has truly given up trying to be lovable! This is why therapy for actualization and realness requires something more than motivated striving and simple conditioning. It requires being able to discover the wealth of personal growth that comes from giving up and surrendering to growth instead of merely striving for it. The four characteristics of actualization have this paradoxical quality. They can be striven for by engaging in a process, but the process requires that the patient give up trying to be them!

Omnipotence or Humanness?

The manipulator never has learned the secret of balance between authentic surrender and honest striving. He is instead a Junior God who tries to run his life and others by control and manipulation. He has a deeply rooted attitude of distrust in himself and others. Even his passive, helpless manipulations are a form of striving for omnipotence in that the helpless one always controls and directs the active ones in his life. His active demanding and "shoulding" are also forms of omnipotence that deeply distrust the potential for independent action on the part of the other person. The manipulator tries to hide what he feels is the ugly or manipulative side of his paradoxical nature.

Actualization is the alternative which offers humanness, of believing in oneself and one's full *potentials* and at the same time valuing one's *limitations* and loving oneself in spite of these limitations. The actualizor swings with his inner scale of balance between his polarities. In a very profound sense, the actualizor is a deeply religious person who believes that his organism, as made, can be trusted to work and that he will swing effectively back and forth between his complimentary potentials in his effort to cope with the problems of living.

Awareness

Possibly the most important idea I can leave with you is that man need not be a manipulator and, equally important, need not be a hopeless victim of manipulation. *With awareness, manipulation decreases, and actualization increases.*

A basic procedure from Gestalt therapy, which helps us in this regard, is the concept of the "continuum of awareness." This means that one can learn to focus on the ever-changing moment and simply express what he is experiencing from moment to moment in his awareness. What we focus on at the moment seems to be summarized in three dimensions: (1) Here vs. There (Someplace else); (2) Now vs. Past or Future; (3) Feelings vs. Thinking or Sensing.

The therapist, in helping a patient learn how to become

101

aware, constantly directs him to finish this statement: "Here and now I am aware that—." The patient picks it up here and describes what he is feeling, thinking, and sensing in the here and now. His thinking consists either of remembering the past or planning the future; his sensing is what he is now seeing or hearing; his feeling is the emotion he is experiencing at the time. Consider the following conversation, for example.

Therapist: Finish the statement, "Here and now I am aware that. . . ."

Patient: Here and now I am aware that I am afraid.

Therapist: Can you describe *where* you are feeling your fear?

Patient: My voice is weak, and my hands are wet and clammy.

Therapist: What else are you aware of?

Patient: I am aware of the air conditioning noise in the room.

Therapist: What else are you aware of?

Patient: I'm aware of the rough texture of this chair arm.

Therapist: Where are you feeling the roughness?

Patient: I am aware of the roughness on the palm of my hand.

Therapist: Are you aware that you are kicking your leg?

Patient: I am aware that I am kicking my leg.

Therapist: Who would you like to kick?

Patient: You, for making me do these silly exercises.

This example illustrates the importance of learning to be aware of the *obvious*. The manipulator customarily does not see or hear such small things as movements of his hands and feet, facial expressions, posture, and intonation of voice in himself or others. As he is led to increase his awareness through exercises such as the one illustrated here, he moves from deadness to aliveness. Instead of relying on his deliberate calculations as a manipulator, he is helped to trust his spontaneous reactions to his world.

Why is awareness so important? Awareness, it is often said, is the goal of psychotherapy. The reason is that *change occurs with awareness!* Awareness is a form of non-striving achieved by being what you are at the moment, even if it means the phony manipulative role that we all play sometimes for external support.

In the safety of a therapeutic situation, one can critically experience these manipulative roles, no matter how silly, foolish, or ridiculous they may be. One then experiences their self-defeating quality and becomes free to create from these roles the complimentary actualizing behaviors. The latter will be experienced instead as creative, since they will have support from within, rather than from without. Awareness of the futility of manipulative strivings leads naturally to the centered power of self-actualization. The road to emotional health is through expression of manipulative behaviors, not through rejection and striving for change!

The following example taken from therapy will illustrate:

Therapist: What are you aware of now?

Patient: I'm aware of wanting to hit you.

Therapist: Be the you that wants to hit.

Patient: I want to hit you because you won't decide for me.

Therapist: Now be me and answer that.

Patient: "Gloria, you will never grow up if you keep getting me to make your decisions."

Therapist: And what do you answer?

Patient: You are right, darn you!

By asking the patient to experience her dependent manipulation and then by asking her to be the "wise therapist," the therapist gets her to discover and respect her own wise actualizing potential which lies naturally deep within herself.

NOTES

1. Leo Tolstoy.
2. Gene Sagar, unpublished manuscript.
3. Erich Fromm, *The Heart of Man*, ed. by Ruth N. Ashen (New York: Harper & Row, 1964), pp. 52, 132.
4. Abraham H. Maslow, *Motivation and Personality* (New York: Harper & Row, 1954), p. 222.
5. *Ibid.*, p. 291.
6. See *The Neurotic Personality of Our Time* (New York: W. W. Norton & Company, 1937), pp. 270-75.
7. *The Search for Authenticity*, p. 209.
8. Marie Robinson, *The Power of Sexual Surrender* (New York: Doubleday & Company, 1959), pp. 209-12.
9. Alan W. Watts, *The Wisdom of Insecurity* (New York: Random House, 1949), pp. 9-10.
10. "Faces of Envy," *Review of Existential Psychology and Psychiatry*, I (Spring, 1961), 134-35.

CHAPTER 8
Personal Control

Before we go on to see how the theories of this section are applied to life situations in Part II, I would like to suggest an ethic for the natural control of our behavior which can serve as a backdrop for the life situations we will be discussing.

As shown in Figure 1, man's nature is characterized by many bipolarities. He is active and passive, strong but weak, independent yet dependent, affectionate yet aggressive. He is both top dog and under dog. Now we introduce two more general terms, conservative and liberal.

These terms are chosen because of their universal usage and because of their nonmoralistic connotations. The two-party system in a democracy is a good example of the importance of giving credence to opposing viewpoints. In Great Britain, as we know, the party out of power is referred to as "Her Majesty's Loyal Opposition." In every one of us there is a similar two-party system, each with its loyal opposition, sometimes in power and sometimes not.

You may have used terms like the Strong Me and Weak Me, the Right Me and the Wrong Me; the Real Me and the Unreal Me. All are there inside us every moment of our lives, much as we might wish manipulatively to recognize only the ones we like best.

I use the terms "liberal" and "conservative" to describe these several "me's" because they imply the truth, which is that both are parts of a potential unity. Too often, people would repress or destroy one side or the other of this polarity. The truth is that ultimate mental health requires retaining, valuing and living with both sides of ourselves.

The two sides of our psychological nature may be thought of as parallel to the two sides of physical nature. We have right and left eyes, right and left ears, right and left arms, and so on. Recently a patient came to see me, complaining that her husband was unfaithful; she was afraid he was about to leave her and wanted me to save the marriage. As she talked, almost immediately I observed that it was as if the left side of her body was paralyzed. All her gestures, for instance, were with her right hand. Her left hand lay limply in her lap. I learned that she was a very conservative person, a kindergarten teacher for over twenty years, who habitually did nothing to displease anyone. She had been referred to me by her family physician, who said she had no physical ailment.

As we talked, I requested that she make her gestures with her left hand, instead of the right. Initially she found this quite difficult. It became clear that her entire orientation was "right." She always did the "right thing," said the "right thing," and never expressed a "different" point of view. In effect she was dull and lifeless. Little wonder her husband found her uninteresting.

It is said that an art student can learn to "seduce" his right hand to more expressiveness by drawing with the left. Use of the left hand seems to release the right hand to greater freedom. Therapy for this woman, then, is to help impart new life to her thinking and hence her body, which had become as rigid, stiff, and unresponsive as her thinking. When she is free to express both sides of her nature, which I describe as her conservative and liberal sides, she will be more interesting to her husband and herself.

I am not saying that conservatism means complete control and liberality means complete license. Rather, I'm saying that when we use both eyes and ears, we see and hear in depth, stereophonically. The actualizing person dances between his right and left complimentary polarities, and in this process there is natural restraint, rather than artificial restraint as manifested by the behavior of our uninteresting schoolteacher.

Suppose we regard our organism as a dynamic, ever-changing unit, yet bipolar in its potential for expression.

This may be seen more clearly in the form of a teeter-totter:

A person in balance is one whose teeter-totter is moving continually in dynamic interplay between his convervative and liberal potentials. One side of the teeter-totter goes up, and that side comes into awareness; the needs of that side of his nature predominate. Circumstances change, and the other end of his personal teeter-totter goes up. As long as he continues to live by the law of *expression*—expressing what he *feels* by behavior, fantasy, or verbal expression—then the individual will continue to move in organismic balance. Neither conservative nor liberal tendencies will predominate or become fixated.

One of the basic needs of every person is to take responsibility for his own balance. As a suggested ethic, *responsibility in this sense means accepting responsibility for one's self and one's own natural rhythmic balance, not depending on anyone else to establish controls for behavior.* We all have liberal and conservative sides. The conservative *must* accept his liberal side just as the liberal *must* accept his conservative side. In the open expression of both sides of his nature, the individual has a natural means by which to live his life with greatest ease, which affords great challenge and still a minimum of artificial controls imposed from without.

External systems of morality may be seen as blankets of

artificial control which are required to keep immature people from behaving unwisely. As parents and spouses, we feel we need to impose such systems on our children and our mates because, usually, we really do not trust our *own* organismic balance and therefore cannot trust the balance of those we love.

An internal system of bipolar expression is, of course, the alternative to the external system of control. This has been described as a system of *organismic self-regulation*. Instead of simply controlling or breaking one's natural expression, man focuses instead on an understanding of his potentialities. Perls writes:

> I have still to see a case of nervous breakdown which is not due to over-control, and to its aggravation by the nagging of friends to "pull yourself together." The example of a motor car suggests itself. The motor car has many controls. The brakes are only one of them, and the crudest at that. The better the driver understands how to handle all the controls, the more efficiently will the car function. But if he drives with the brakes permanently on, the wear and tear on the brake and engine will be enormous; the performance of the car will deteriorate, and sooner or later there will be a breakdown. The better the driver understands a car's potentialities, the better he can control it and the less will he mishandle it. The over-controlled person behaves in exactly the same way as the ignorant driver. He knows no other means of control than the brakes—than repressions.[1]

The actualizor would be seen then as a person who is aware of both his strengths and weaknesses and, therefore, does not project either of them excessively onto others. He is aware that there is always a parallel between inner and outer—how we feel about ourselves and others.

109

The manipulator, on the other hand, being a person excessively fixated or preoccupied with his own strengths or weaknesses, *denies* or *disowns* those parts of himself which he cannot accept as internal.

We see the manipulative businessman admitting to his therapist that he has strong sexual desires for his secretary. Projecting his inner conservative self—his conscience and feelings of restraint—onto his wife, he makes himself feel controlled and unhappy, feeling only his inner sex feeling. If the businessman could be honest with himself, a therapist might tell him to imagine that he has in himself both liberal and conservative views on this issue and ask him to express that inner dialogue.

Therapist:	*Be* your inner feelings about this.
Businessman:	I want that woman, and I don't care what it costs.
Therapist:	Okay. Now *be* your conservative feelings.
Businessman:	I don't have any conservative feelings.
Therapist:	I think you do. Wait for your conservative self to talk.
Businessman:	(Long pause) Hmmm. Well I guess it says, "Are you sure you would pay any price?"
Therapist:	And what does the liberal side say to that?
Businessman:	"Well, almost any price, so long as I don't hurt anybody."
Therapist:	And the conservative side?

Businessman: "What makes you think you won't hurt anybody? Especially yourself?"

Therapist: The liberal answer to that?

Businessman: The liberal side says, "I guess there's always some kind of price."

The dialogue could be continued, but our purpose is to illustrate that the actualizing person is one who takes, embraces, and accepts ownership of his internal bipolarity while the manipulator projects and blames others. Let's look in on a college student in therapy.

Student: I get so damned mad at my father always demanding I stay in school.

Therapist: Let's make believe that your father is sitting over there. Now you say what he would say.

Student: Father says, "You'll just never get a decent job if you quit school."

Therapist: And what do you say?

Student: I'm going in the Army anyhow. Why can't I have some fun until I do?

Therapist: And Father says?

Student: "You don't know how soon you're going in the Army. You could use the time you have to learn as much as you can."

Therapist: And you say?

Student: You always want me to work and never let me have fun.

Therapist: Father says?

Student: "I want you to work so you can have fun."

Therapist: Who really said that?

Student: . . . Damn you! (Student becomes aware
                that the father projected "out there" is
                really his own inner feeling of conserva-
                tism.)

The Role of Religion

A word needs to be said here about the place of religion in guiding human behavior.[2] A manipulative religion is one that stresses the inability of man to trust his
own nature. If he cannot trust his own nature, he needs
some external religious system. An actualized religion is
one that stresses that the kingdom of God is within and
that trusting one's nature is the highest form of religion,
in that one is trusting God's handiwork. The role of
religion in the first sense is to keep man more like a helpless child who constantly needs the external help of ministers and priests. The role of religion in the actualized
sense is to foster self-direction and self-growth. An external
religion then becomes more and more internal. Thus, the
actualizing minister, priest or rabbi, is seen by the actualizing person as less a judge and answer-giver and more
of a resource person, sharing and growing together with
his parishioner. He is a consultant, not a Junior God!

To conclude this discussion of ethics is a message from
a poet with an introspective turn of mind:

> Within my earthly temple there's a crowd;
> There's one of us that's humble, one that's proud,
> There's one that's broken-hearted for his sins,
> And one that unrepentant sits and grins;

There's one that loves his neighbors as himself,
And one that cares for naught but fame and pelf,
From much corroding care I should be free
If I could once determine which is me! [3]

An actualizing person, of course, knows the two crowds within and is willing to accept each in the creative fellowship of self.

NOTES

1. *Ego, Hunger and Aggression*, p. 224.
2. The whole idea of manipulation and actualization in religion is explored at greater length with two ministers, Maxie Dunnam and Gary Herbertson, in *The Manipulator and the Church* (Nashville: Abingdon Press, 1968).
3. Edward Stanford Martin, "Mixed."

PART III
Examples of Manipulation
and Actualization

CHAPTER 9

Children and Parents

Yes, children are often manipulators too. Like most of modern man, they come in the usual number of recognizable packages.

Types of Manipulative Children

The first type is the "Little Weakling." He drags his feet and tries to make us do his work for him. This passive, dependent child manipulates us with his very helplessness and indecisiveness, his chronic forgetting and stalling. Discovering early in life the power in appearing ineffectual, he "plays" helpless and stupid, the helplessness getting him special attention until the pattern is stamped into him. He isn't just lazy, as many of us think. He is "stupid like a fox" because he is clever enough to manipulate the adults in his life to do everything for him.

The second type of child manipulator is active, and we know him as the "Little Dictator." He controls the adults in his life by pouting, stubbornness, procrastination, and inefficiency, and by stamping his feet, he tries to make us do his work for him. He's always "busy"—hasn't time for chores—uses tantrums, nagging, pouting, and all manner of irritating techniques to wear us down.

The development of these two fundamental types of manipulator has been discussed early in this book. Let's look now at several other examples as they apply to children.

1. "Freddy-the-Fox" started life as a crier and spent his first six weeks on earth getting practice at it. Tears, he found, paid off in attention. He hadn't even begun to think, or reason, mind you, and then he got a skin rash which produced more of that tender loving care. He didn't run into real opposition to his wishes until he had to get out and mix with society in school. By then and unconsciously to be sure, he had the secret weapon. He had become a Junior Calculator. Whenever the lessons seemed too hard, or teacher too exacting, he "cleverly" developed a stomachache that would let him go home. If he didn't dress himself for school, mother did it for him. He got extra attention in school because the teacher felt sorry for him. In fact, he was becoming a master at making people feel

sorry for him. Even other children were seduced by his "hurts" when they played ball. Somehow he always was "hurt" when it paid off. He had also discovered the advantages of being a weakling and clinging vine.

2. "Tom-the-Tough," on the other hand, has a violent temper. He pushes, bangs, and spits on other children. His vocabulary would scare a football player. He likes guns and knives. Early in life he discovered that hate and fear, when mixed, control people—even adults. He had become a Junior Bully. He especially hates authority, either parents or teachers. He has certitude, appearing confident and absolutely sure himself, and he buffaloes everyone. He seems to have a mental hearing aid that turns off at the precise moment teachers or parents open their mouths.

3. "Carl-the-Competitor" is sort of a combination Tom and Freddy. The younger of two boys in his family, he learned early to fight and compete for everything. Since school was competitive, that was his meat. His parents, brothers, and every other student became the "enemy." Winning and being "one-up" became more important than learning itself. Then, this competition began to cripple him, he got straight A's but also insomnia. Other bright students were a perpetual source of fear to him.

The Manipulative Parent

Manipulators aren't born, of course. They are created out of healthy little babies. As they begin to grow into the manipulative world of modern man, the first training they get is from their parents, who are themselves products of our manipulative society.

The manipulative parent sees his job in life as one of

controlling the outward behavior of his children. He has a strong sense of responsibility for them, and this frequently develops into feelings of omnipotence. He plays Judge and God.

This parent's chief verbal approach to the child is "you should." He really believes that manipulating outward behavior is called for and believes further that his Godlike pronouncements will change behavior. His "shoulds" fall into a number of variations—"You can," "You can't," "You don't want to," "You should want to," "If you do, then you can."

One of the prime manipulative techniques of the judging omnipotent parent is to control *by guilty feelings*. If the child doesn't do what he wishes, the parent tries to create guilt feelings in him. A manipulative parent, for instance, would try to shame Freddy-the-Fox out of his childishness by such comments as "Why don't you be a big boy instead of a baby?" To Tom-the-Tough, he would say: "You ought to be ashamed of yourself for hurting other children." To Carl-the-Competitor: "You shouldn't try to win all the time. I'm going to have a heart attack if you keep acting this way." If the parent does have a heart attack, even years later, the son or daughter may be plagued by these deeply planted guilt feelings.

Another device of the manipulative parent is to foster other-directedness. To Freddy, such a parent says, "You don't want people to think you can't do it." To Tom, he says: "What will people think when you use that kind of language?" To Carl, "No one will like you if you keep competing so hard."

The use of love is still a third manipulative device. To a Freddy, the parent says, "I just can't love you when you're so stupid." To Tom, "You couldn't love me, or you wouldn't act this way." She fosters Carl's competitiveness by saying, "I love you so much when you get such good grades." Here the parent plays the Nice Guy manipulation.

Another manipulative technique is the use of expectations. To Freddy, the parent says: "You should be big and strong." Or, "How do you expect to be strong like your father?" To Tom, "I expect you to do as I say" (thus encouraging further rebellion). To Carl, "Everyone in our family has always done well in school."

There are many techniques commonly used by manipulative parents. No doubt you can add a number of your own. Where do they get us? Do they achieve that behavior we want so badly in our offspring? Do they bring that wonderful thing we call discipline?

Methods of Discipline

There is no area of child psychology, perhaps, that is more misunderstood than that of discipline. As an alternative to manipulating our children and their manipulating us, I believe we must all develop some philosophy in this important area. Disciplinary techniques fall into two broad categories. One is an action-centered, manipulative, or control type. The other is characterized by being internal, self-imposed, and actualizing—what we know as self-discipline, in which the child's internalized values are his guiding principles.

Action-centered discipline embodies ideas of reward and punishment, a method still practiced by many well-meaning parents. "Spare the rod and spoil the child," they say. Or, "Children should be seen and not heard." These typical household phrases usually are accompanied by several action-control techniques, all manipulating the child's behavior—verbal punishment, unfavorable comparison, isolation, deprivation of privileges, and physical punishment.

The effect of such punishment actually is to inhibit behavior or repress feelings. Punishment causes anxiety and tends to produce nervous manifestations characteristic of repression. It often arouses hatred for the punisher, counter aggressions, and guilt feelings that result in need for further punishment. Finally, punishment frequently arouses feelings of insecurity and inadequacy. The punished child perceives himself as fallen from the good graces of the punisher and tends to feel more insecure. He has been made to think of himself as bad, incompetent, worthless, and often he acts in terms of these self-pictures.

Action-control methods of discipline assume that punishment leads to reform. The truth is, as studies of criminals show us, that punishment does not prevent or deter antisocial behavior but may actually encourage the very things it sets out to destroy.

Many parents today, having an increasing knowledge of basic psychological principles, no longer are comfortable with manipulative disciplinary methods. They want their children to behave in ways which are both socially acceptable and best for physical and mental health. They are unsure of just how to achieve such behavior, failing to recognize that their demands for respect and obedience often are results of their own insecurity. These parents lack the understanding that hostility expressed by children, within reasonable limits, actually is necessary for their emotional growth.

If a child *feels* secure, adequate, and worthy, there is far less chance that he will be a discipline problem. A reflection of feelings and acceptance meets his need for understanding. Thus we come to actualizing *feeling-centered* discipline as the alternative to *action-centered* control. It has self-control, rather than blind obedience to others, as its goal.

Unfortunately, the feeling approach to discipline cannot be reduced to a set of simple rules, which require punishment if broken. Discipline is much more a matter of attitude and feeling (as are manipulations). The child who is being disciplined must be accepted as a human being—not as an automaton—with rights and feelings of his own. The parent who can handle attitudes and feelings well will also handle discipline problems skillfully. If the emotional climate around the home is generally warm and accepting, the child will feel secure even when firmness is used and when appropriate limits are set in accord with his developmental level.

This feeling-centered approach to discipline requires that attitude be separated from actions and the individual from his actions. A mother or father may be displeased with what his child has *done* (his actions), but their feelings toward him as a person (friendliness, acceptance, love, and approval) needn't change.

A Theory of Discipline

When one disciplines a child, he may do it either in terms of action or in terms of feelings. Parent and child operate on a continuum between these two behaviors. The concept is illustrated in Figure 4. The center line extending downward from actions to attitudes may be described as a continuum from outer observable actions at the top to the more obscure underlying feelings at the bottom. The child being disciplined will exhibit to the parent behavior which falls somewhere on this attitude-action continuum. The underlying principle is that the parent should react to the child at the point on the action-feeling continuum at which the child is himself behaving. For example, if the child is discussing feelings, the parent reflects feelings (the same level); but if the child moves into the action field, the parent then must deal with him at this level.

Figure 4
The Action-Feeling Continuum

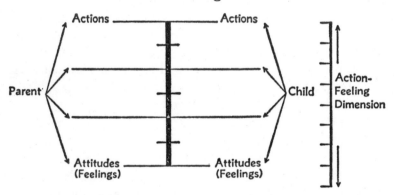

Let's look at several situations in which this is demonstrated.

1. *Attitude only.* A child comes to his parent complaining about his teachers and principal. This activity is in the field of force of the child's feelings and represents only the child's feelings or attitudes on the subject. Therefore, the parent responds according to his own feelings:

Parent: We've found through experience that it isn't good to go around talking about others in the outside world. On the other hand, we do all need a place where we can blow off steam once in a while. So that's what you can do now, if you like.

Child: Sometimes I feel mad enough just to blow the whole school a mile high. They make a guy work and slave, and where does it get him? Another guy comes along and gets the A's because he apple-polishes the teacher. (All this is pure feeling of course.)

Note here, though, that attitude is met with attitude. As long as the child stays in the attitudinal field, the discussion can continue satisfactorily.

2. *Before the act is committed.*

Child: I get so mad at that school I'm going over and break all the windows in the darn place (expressing feeling and contemplating action).

Parent: Well, I certainly see that you feel very strongly about it. Let's see what would happen if you did break the windows.

The child here is moving from the feeling field into the action field. In addition to expressing feeling, he actually is discussing acting out his feelings. The parent has the right to enter the action field at this point. The action he chooses is to structure the consequences of his child's contemplated action. After the action is structured, it may be wise for him to explore further and see if growth is changing the stated desires.

3. *Action has been committed, and punishment is being weighed.* If the child tells of an argument in which he "told off" a friend, this is in the action field. However, it would do no harm to respond to the child's feelings since the "good" or "bad" of his actions are themselves debat-

able without much more knowledge of the incident. It is more important that no injury results to the child or to others. Permissiveness at this point may even enable the child to go ahead with his "catharsis," which he needs before he can look at the situation wisely.

Child: I sure told off Jimmy.

Parent: Well now, suppose you tell me about it. Do you feel you were justified?

4. *Act has been committed, and punishment is required.*

If the parent decides to punish the child, it still is possible for him to remain personally nonjudgmental. Even if the child has committed a misdemeanor, the parent may not feel the need to express his own moral indignation. A parent doesn't need to be a judge but can be an expresser. For instance,

Parent: Son, I called you in because I wanted to discuss the broken windows at the Smith's. Is there anything you want to say about it? I may not be able to help you, but would you like to talk about it? (Here he gives the child a chance to express his feelings.)

Then,

Parent: Well, from what you say, I gather that you feel you aren't entirely responsible. On the other hand, the rules apply here just as in a basketball game when the referee blows the whistle on a foul. What do you think would be a fair punishment in this case?

In this kind of situation the child could discuss his attitudes toward the punishment administered by his parent until it becomes a real growing experience toward self-

126

responsibility. The punishment should, though, be made external to the relationship of parent and child.

The following are principles which might help in this theory of actualizing feeling-centered discipline:

1. Separate the feelings involved from the actions. Be nonjudgmental of the child himself, even though his actions must be judged. Separation of the child from his actions permits the parent to accept him on a genuine friendly basis. The child knows he is liked for himself but that his actions are not acceptable and must be improved. Actions are the result of feelings (rejection and/or hostility). In order to change actions, the feelings first must be understood and handled.

2. Study the child and determine whether you are dealing with a normal or neurotic child. In the disturbed youngster the action must be considered as a symptom of much deeper emotional difficulty, probably caused originally by criticism, rejection, blame, or earlier punishment. To impose punishment arbitrarily in such a case simply would cause this child to become more disturbed.

3. Accept and reflect the child's feelings. Arrange conditions so the child can let off steam, "blow up," or otherwise safely release the hostile feelings which he has been trying to suppress.

4. If punishment is required, allow the child to suggest what he thinks would be a fair and reasonable punishment for his actions. Experienced parents tell us that the child usually will recommend more severe punishment for himself than that which ordinarily would be imposed by the authority figure.

5. If punishment must be imposed, be certain the child realizes that it is his action of breaking a rule that brings it. Help him to see that rules have been established for

group conduct and must be obeyed just as the rules of a basketball game must be binding upon all of the players.

6. Work with the child on discipline as a mutual problem. Let him know that you feel it is a mutual problem, not just his own. This suggests the idea of separating the problem both from the child and parent, temporarily setting it out at a distance where both can examine and work on it together. Suggesting that the problem has an external reference point enables the child to refrain from making the discipline situation an interpersonal conflict.

7. Limits must be placed on dangerous and destructive actions. Permit an expression of feeling; then assist the child to rechannel actions which cannot be allowed. This is the basic formula for a dynamic approach to discipline.

The Actualizing Parent

In contrast to the manipulative parent, the actualizing mother or father is *growth* oriented. He sees his place in life as working himself out of a job. Instead of being *should* oriented, he is *is* oriented. He tries to accept his child as he is and endeavors to help him grow from there. His chief aim always is to foster self-actualization in the child. This parent does not see life as a child's world, or as an adult's world, but rather as a *person's* world, where every individual has the right to satisfy his own needs. Let's see how the actualizing parent might treat our three problem type lads, Freddy, Tom, and Carl.

With Freddy-the-Fox, the actualizing parent sees Freddy's "is-ness" as one of prolonged dependency, weakness, and calculation (See Figure 1). Her job, as she sees it, is to help Freddy develop the opposites of these. So the actualizing parent encourages Freddy to do various independent tasks: go to the store, make his bed, handle money, dress himself. Independent behavior is rewarded with warmth and praise; for example, "Daddy, did you hear that Freddy dressed himself today?" His *dependency* is thus turned into an appreciation of himself by his parents' valuing of his independent behavior.

Effort is made also to turn Freddie's using *weakness* into *empathic* understanding, and his *calculations* into *respecting* behavior. This is done by allowing him to have a dog, by calling his attention to sick children in the hospital, attending to neighbors' needs, etc.

With Tom-the Tough, the actualizing parent attempts to actualize the affection and support potentials to counteract the overly developed hate and fear she sees in Tom's bullying. She recognizes his hostility toward other children as a desire not to be overlooked and a feeling of loss of support and caring. Mother, father, and teacher all will have to cooperate in a program of appreciation for what he does right, rather than emphasize what he does wrong. They demonstrate for him an actualizing certitude which is born of inner self-support rather than the need to impress outwardly.

With Carl-the-Competitor, the actualizing parent focuses on the development of self-support, a healthy trust, and dependency on others. The parents help Carl to see that competitiveness develops out of a lack of trust in self and a need for some outer standard to fight against. They teach him, like General Eisenhower, to "shoot against his own par," rather than against the scores of others.

The Actualization-Centered Approach

A philosophy of child rearing can help all of us with children and, at the same time, give us self-respect as parents is an "actualization-centered" approach. Look at it this way, if you will:

Figure 5
The Shift in Responsibility

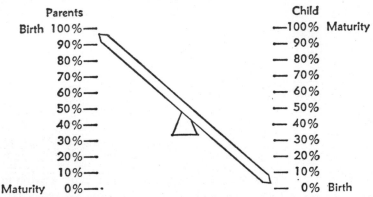

From *The Dynamics of the Counseling Process* by E. L. Shostrom and L. M. Brammer. Copyright 1952 by the McGraw-Hill Book Company. Used by permission of the McGraw-Hill Book Company.

At birth, a child is in a stage of utter helplessness. Unless his parents, and especially his mother, take full charge of his life, he will die. His training begins at birth and should be oriented constantly toward the kind of atmosphere in which he will become increasingly *self*-responsible and his parents increasingly *less* responsible for his life. Somewhere along the line, perhaps at age eleven or twelve, the balance of responsibility between parent and child should be equal. At what age should we expect the balance of power to be reversed completely? At about the time of graduation from high school, around eighteen to twenty-one, the young person should be self-responsible and able to take care of himself in the world.

The goal of our actualization-centered approach to raising children is, of course, their actualization into adulthood. The parallel growth of the parent should never be relinquished in the process. The actualizing parent should see himself also in the process of growing, of being human and fallible and wanting the full life. His needs and feelings must always be equally important to those of the child.

The Actualizing Parents' Bill of Rights

1. Cooperate with us; don't remain younger than you are by "playing" helpless and stupid. Give us the feeling that we can grow together and that we can count on you to become eventually independent of us.

2. Remember that firm teaching means business. Maybe you need to assert your independence by saying "No," but we have our *limits*.

3. We are trying to work ourselves out of a job as parents with you, but we need you to develop response-ability—the ability to respond!

4. We are trying to reduce our *shoulds*, but remember that it's your job to develop wholesome *wants* to replace them.

5. The only consistent thing about adults or *humans*, because we are *fallible*, is that we are inconsistent. Accept our *fall*-ability too.

6. We'd like you to tell us you appreciate us, too, when we please you. "Thanks" spurs me on!

7. Accept our rules sometimes even if you don't under-

stand them. Being adults, we really do sometimes know best!

8. Don't always expect answers from us. Understanding the question is more important than knowing answers.

9. Remember that we'd also like your interest in our activities. Adults aren't *always* square, and you may learn to like some of what we do.

10. Love us when you think for sure we are wrong. Being a parent isn't being God—even if you demand omnipotence, we are really just human.

11. Our examples may not always please you. Don't copy us exactly, be creatively *you*.

12. Remember to respond to us as equals too. Parents are not slaves to children; we need fairness also.

13. We need fun too. Respect our friends as we respect yours. Our activities may seem dull to you, but we have a right to have them.

14. Our home belongs to *all* of us. Things aren't as important as people, but try to learn to respect the things which people prize.

15. We want you as junior partners in our family firm, but remember not to treat us as if we are *retired*. We still have an active role in the company!

16. Make your own decisions wisely, and we will love you *in spite of* the fact that we know they won't always be wise!

17. Parents also grow as parents in stages. We will be smarter a few years from now. Let's all pull together instead of pulling apart.

P.S. We Love You!

CHAPTER 10
Teen-Agers

Five minutes after the woman sat down across from my desk, I knew that her problem was not one of being a failing parent but one of not being an aware parent. She was not aware of the necessary "divorce" that must take place between every actualizing teen-ager and his parents. It is the most common, and least understood, problem of parents of teen-agers today.

133

After one hour's chat, this worried mother decided to quit taking the advice of her neighbors to "lay down the law" and be more strict. Instead, she resolved to compliment her young man for his increasing independence, to "give him up" to adulthood rather than keeping him a child, and to find new interests for herself to fill the vacuum.

Her fifteen-year-old wasn't, after all, too different from most teen-agers. His mode of rebellion was individual with him, but need for rebellion is a universal adolescent need. He wore his hair longer than another generation considers pleasing. Pleasing parents, after all, is "square" and taboo. He was spending most of his waking hours away from home with his peer group, other teen-agers whom his mother considered undesirable. Communication was nil. There was virtually no dialogue between him and his parents. Defiantly keeping them out of his shell, his attitude, indeed his expression, was: "So what?"

In the family of man, there is really nothing new in this. It is only new to those parents who are going through it, and that's what causes the panic. Where have we gone wrong? Why is this happening to us? Where will it all end —in the reform school with us bringing cookies on Sunday?

Of course not.

The paradox is that the prescription is for this parent to do nothing rather than something. This is just a natural stage of development. He'll grow out of it. My counsel to ninety percent of such worried parents is very simple: "Love them and let them grow."

Essentially this is the same old story of the prodigal son who is cured by the patience of the waiting father. The prodigal usually comes to himself in the course of time unless the anxious parent, in his concern, delays the process. To me, the story of the prodigal son is really that of the waiting and patient parent. Don't forget the elder brother who never rebelled and therefore remained an immature and jealous child.

In the frenzy of this frightened age, we have been hearing many alarming comments on the "tragedy of our teenagers." This flood of anxiety has brought many parents to seek professional help. I found it helpful finally to compile lists of the most common ways in which these two groups of human beings, who actually love each other, habitually attempt to manipulate one another. I would like to offer them here since, to one degree or another, they illustrate the ever-present conflict between parents and teeners.

Teen Ways of Manipulating Parents

1. *Crying.* When they want something, they whine or cry.

2. *Threatening.* "I'm gonna sign up for the service." "Guess I'll quit school." "I might just get married." "I might get into trouble."

3. *You don't love me or you would—.*

4. *Comparing.* "Nobody gets his hair cut short." "Bill's father bought him a new Mustang." "*Every*one has a cashmere sweater." "Those kids don't have to wash every five minutes." "*Every*body else is going."

5. *Blackmailing.* "I'll probably get sick." "You know I spill things when we go out to dinner." "I'll tell Dad you've been hiding that bill from him."

6. *Playing one parent against the other.* "Mother

135

won't let me go—you will, won't you?" "Dad won't let me have the car—you ask him for me."

7. *Lying.* "We're going to the library" (not mentioning the party five minutes afterward). "I wasn't really involved. I know who took it, but I didn't."

8. *Moping.* Depressed; causing mother to do what he wants in order to cheer him up.

Parent Manipulations of Teen-Agers

1. *Dangling apples.* "Do the yard, and I'll get you a credit card." "Take out the trash, and I'll increase your allowance." "I have two tickets to the baseball game; be good and we'll see how it works out."

2. *Threats.* "If you don't drive Aunt Agnes, you'll be walking too." "I guess I'll have to go to school and see how your grades are." "So long as we pay the bills around here, you'll shape up."

3. *Comparisons.* "John doesn't get as much allowance as you do now." "Bill does better in school than you." "I like your friend Tom; he's so courteous."

4. *Making insincere promises.* "You can go to Disneyland some day." "I'll talk to that man about flying lessons." "I want you to have one of those sweaters."

5. *Blackmailing.* "I'll tell Dad on you when he gets home." "Your teacher wouldn't be happy to know how little time you give your homework."

6. *Illness as a control.* "If you don't stop that, I'll have a heart attack." "You'll simply have to quiet down; I think I'm getting a migraine."

7. *Using Love.* "You wouldn't do this if you loved me."

All these practices suggest that a real "game" is going on between teen-agers and adults. The parents, being legally responsible, are the top dogs, while the teener, feeling himself the under dog, is ready to manipulate in every possible way. An all-out manipulative battle is the inevitable result. Further, since the teen-agers keep slipping out of the patterns adults impose on them, the adults feel they must resort to power plays. The first rule of the parent, therefore, is that all this is very serious and not really a game. The teen-agers also feel it's serious and are determined to "win."

For purposes of clarity, let us view the struggle between teens and adults as a contest wherein, from the rebellious teen point of view, the rule is: "I win, you lose." Teens look at the whole situation from this assumption. To them, parents are competitors or enemies to be won over. Every encounter between teen and parent thereafter is at least a minor skirmish.

Examples

Sally is leaving for school on a chilly morning, wearing only a light jacket. "I want you to wear a coat," says Mother. "That jacket's much too light." Comes now the teen reply: "I don't want to wear a coat." And the adult reply: "I am your mother, and you will do what I say. You will wear a coat." Sally says flatly: "I will not." Now the enemies are locked in battle.

If Mother wins, the teen-ager feels angry, sulks, and goes off to classes mad at all adults, perhaps scheming how to punish the entire family as well as the school. Maybe she wears the coat, but only until she is three blocks from home, when she removes it. If the youngster wins in this undeclared war, Mother sulks. She may "chew out" Father for not making his daughter behave and go on to have a thoroughly bad day.

Thus we see how the parent also assumes the "I win-you lose" attitude. Mother has said, in effect, "Because I am legally responsible and you are immature, you will play the game by my rules." Her exaggerated sense of responsibility becomes a form of omnipotence.

Suppose, though, that Mother has learned to actualize the game. If she could convince herself first of all, and secondarily her teen-ager, that the model of living need not be a battle, but friendship or a mutuality of sharing, a whole new approach might be made. If, furthermore, she understood the principle of synergy, as Maslow uses it, she would play the game in an actualizing, rather than manipulative or competitive way. The principle of synergy states that it is possible for people who are actualizing to come to a point at which they can genuinely open their being in company with another and see that that which they seek is also most often meaningful to the other.

Mother, for example, would remind herself: We are not enemies; we are friends, and with friends the rule is *when you win, I win—when you lose, I lose*. If we can assume that we are friends (her reasoning continues), then we can agree that our needs are not different. "Can we both agree that we don't want you to catch cold?" she asks. "Okay, now we differ only in our solutions. You feel you needn't wear the coat to keep from catching cold. I do. Let's look at the alternatives. What can we do instead?"

With this approach Sally well may answer: "Well, how about wearing a sweater under my jacket?"

"Fine," says Mother.

What has happened here? The rules of the game have been altered, obviously. Mother and Sally are operating now on a friendly, problem-solving basis. In problem-solving we first agree on a common goal, explore alternative solutions and their consequences, and, finally, agree on one of the alternatives. Instead of being enemies or competitive manipulators out to win over one another, we are engaged in a friendly, problem-solving process.

Naturally, because of many factors, a solution to Mother's and Sally's problem might not have worked out as smoothly as this. Nevertheless, the solution usually will be successful if it is based on the idea of mutual respect. If the mother can treat her youngster as an equal rather than as an inferior, she might even let her wear only the jacket so that she will learn by the natural consequences of suffering from the cold. Risk-taking is part of learning and growing. Suffering is too.

We all could avoid a lot of our troubles if we only would understand the concepts of winning and losing. Winning and losing are hypotheses of how life works, and they are false concepts. Perls has stated, "Whenever we win, we lose; and whenever we lose, we win." This describes life more as it really is.

Too many parents think of themselves as experts on the lives of their children, and their approach unfortunately is a "shoulding" one. Karen Horney describes it as the "Tyranny of the Shoulds." [1] An interesting test is to listen to a parent talk to the child for a few minutes and notice how many times the word "should" is used. Many conversations between parents and children are no more than a string of shoulds.

The alternative to "shouldism" is "is-ism." Rather than

striving for perfection, which raises feelings of impotency and inferiority, we might try to accept life *as it is* and strive for *individual development*. Instead of creating a hell for our children by upholding impossible standards of behavior, we should grow together through creative problem-solving. Only when a person grows can he ultimately assume responsibility for himself.

Let us look at another example of the teen-parent conflict and see how this theory works. Jim is embattled with Dad over his homework. He doesn't want to do it now. He wants to go out first with his club friends for a few hours. "Do your homework now," says Dad, "and then go out." Assuming friendship rather than enemyhood, he adds: "Let's see if we can agree on our goals. We both want to see you finish high school, I believe, and that means finishing homework on time, right?" Jim agrees to that, and Dad asks: "When would you do it, if not now?"

"Well," says Jim, "Suppose I get up early in the morning if it's too late when I get back from club meeting."

"OK," Dad agrees. "We'll try it. But if you don't get up, then next month you'll realize you can't do both and you'll have to give up the club. You've got to learn by experience, apparently." Certainly a tryout like this is better than the continuing conflict which leads to actual blows in some homes.

In still another instance Mary and her parents are in disagreement about her dating. She is only thirteen and wants to go out Friday night with Jack, who is sixteen, to a drive-in movie. Her parents don't want her to date alone in a car yet. "You don't even want me to go to the movies," protests Mary manipulatively. Mother very sensibly replies: "That isn't true. We do want you to go to the movies. It's just that we feel you ought not to leave yourself open to sexual involvement. You make the decision by the way you set up your date. Once you are parked in the orange grove, it may be too late. You lose your freedom to decide because your body takes over. You've got to look at the consequences of every choice."

Mary still argues, "You just don't trust me," she pouts.

Now Dad speaks up: "No, it's just that we don't trust this kind of situation."

So what are the alternatives? After arguing some more, several alternatives emerge: (1) Go to a regular walk-in movie by bus; (2) Dad drives them; (3) Jack's parents drive them; or (4) They go with an older couple, her brother and his girl friend. Ultimately, Mary chooses that.

Some will say that this involves too open an expression of the parents' feelings, but honesty is a prime requisite for actualizing behavior. Don't suppose that it will always be this easy, either. Try to remember that we need principles other than competitiveness and enemyhood on which to work.

Actualizing Parent-Adolescent Relationships

The primary goal of the actualizing parent, as he realizes, is to help the teen-ager channel his feelings into constructive activities. This generation of parents understands that rebellious behavior is a necessary part of growth and that the rebellious teen-ager is rebelling because he trusts the object of his rebellion—his parents—to understand and love him in spite of his rebellion. He cannot trust rebelling against just anyone. Actualizing parents understand that the adolescent is trying to adapt in his own individual way. Consequently, it is unwise for them to force patterns of adulthood on him, and he is permitted to grow at his own individual rate. Actualizing parents have a concept of growth from within, instead of a forced growth from without.

Dorothy Baruch has suggested three things parents need to give their adolescents: understanding, practical sex information, and help in becoming an independent person.[2]

Understanding is difficult without acceptance. As the youth is allowed to express his feelings without fear, the actualizing parent attempts to accept his right to talk back. Too many parents view this as threatening. Such parents, of course, can't understand their child's feelings because they have not first understood their own. This is one of the reasons it is so necessary that parents enter therapy with the adolescent. As the parent learns to talk out his own true feelings with his youngster, he learns to understand both himself and the teen-ager.

The actualizing parent understands that youth needs help in learning to express his feelings and to control his actions. He suggests ways of channeling these negative feelings into socially acceptable actions: (1) verbalize the grievance; (2) write out negative feelings; (3) draw, paint, model, or dramatize; (4) Play games such as tennis, golf, checkers, or chess in order to work out family or peer battles.[3]

Thus, parents who are actualizing realize that their adolescent's feelings, both present and past, cause him to act the way he does. Behind the unacceptable actions are negative feelings which may have had their origin in early childhood. These have come not only from what actually happened but are tied up with the youngster's fantasy of what happened. This imagined fantasy also plays a part in the imagined attitude of the parent toward the youth. If a child felt a lack of love and trust or a sense of belonging in his early life, he tends to find it difficult in adolescence to feel at home with his peers.

To help his teen-ager avoid dangerous behavior is one of the goals of the actualizing parent. This may be accomplished in two ways. First, the parent may anticipate certain interests and provide opportunities for the needed activity with a structured environment: camping, fishing, ball leagues, hot-rod clubs, hunting trips. Secondly, the parent accepts the youth's negative feelings and verbalizes them back to him. When the parent can accept the negative feelings, it is easier for the adolescent to accept them also, thus eliminating guilt feelings.

Sometimes, to be sure, actualizing parents complain: "What about me? I have feelings, too." They know, however, that it is necessary for them also to *express* feelings. So they express their anger and, if they have regrets, say so in sincere humility. The actualizing parent is not surprised at his adolescent's understanding and acceptance when he, as a parent, admits to a problem too. This de-idolization goes a long way toward building rapport between a parent and child and building a teen-ager's respect for his parents' feelings.

Actualizing parents know that limits on adolescent behavior still are necessary. Youth must learn to accept the necessity of certain customs and rules. Baruch has suggested three reasons for limits that can be understood by the adolescent: (1) it is important for health and safety;

143

(2) it is important to protect property; (3) it is important because of law and order and social acceptability.[4]

The Actualizing Teen-Ager

Despite the dropouts who have not found the meaning of long-range goals—the young narcotics addicts who are searching for an easy way and the "tough guy" whose delinquency gives an air of daring bravado—most teen-agers aren't a bad lot. Less than two percent ever break a law. Their music is unintelligible to most adults, but to them it is realistic, as opposed to the themes of fulfillment and romance of the days when present adults were teen-agers. Imperfection and disillusionment are major themes now. Bob Dylan's quote, "The only beauty's ugly, man," gives us a clue. There is a general feeling that they live in a world of loudness, freeways, and jets, where quiet and privacy are found only in the midst of sound.[5] The older generation's emphasis on sports, dates, and laughing at "eggheads" is out. Today's top group manages to be athletes, "A" students, committee chairmen, class officers, and the most socially sought-after.

In the struggle for self-actualization the teen years are the hardest of all. It is surprising that more teeners don't fight it with more manipulative devices and even more antisocial behavior.

Let us, then, examine characteristics of the actualizing teen-ager in terms of three general descriptive categories of any actualizing person: creativity, interpersonal sensitivity, and awareness.

1. *Creativity.* The actualizing teen-ager is a creative rebel. He has the courage to rebel in a healthy manner. His rebellion is not expressed by outward symbols such

as long hair, tight pants, boots, and such, but by purpose, direction, and meaning in his individual behavior. Thus, his rebellion is creative rather than destructive or negative.

2. *Interpersonal sensitivity.* He is not only aware of the feelings of his peers, but is empathic with his parents and other adults. His dress reflects his sensitivity to the occasion.

3. *Awareness.* He wants to enjoy today fully, to experience and have fun, though he is tuned in to the adult world as well. He has a sense of history and goal orientation but still lives fully in the here and now. He is the surfer, for example, who not only enjoys his board but the power of the waves, the bite of the wind, the texture of the sand, and the vastness of the sea.

The teen-ager, as all of us, is a manipulator who is trying to grow into an actualizor. The major job of the parent, it seems to me, is to step out of the way and let it happen.

Notes

1. Karen Horney, *Neuroses and Human Growth* (New York: W. W. Norton & Company, 1950).
2. Dorothy W. Baruch, *How to Live with Your Teen-Ager* (New York: McGraw-Hill Book Company, 1953).
3. *Ibid.,* p. 69.
4. *Ibid.,* p. 11.
5. See R. L. Williams, ed., *The Young Americans* (New York: Time-Life Books, 1966), p. 70.

CHAPTER 11
Lovers

The game of love is as old as man.

Indeed, ever since Adam and Eve, the sexes have haggled over who really was responsible for Adam's eating the apple. Eve seems to get most of the blame for using seductive techniques to manipulate him into the act, but this overlooks the whole moral of the tale, that until he ate and was exposed to the Tree of Knowledge and sin, both were blameless.

146

Certainly the love game didn't start until woman was on the scene with her wiles, but neither could it continue down through the ages without man. It takes two to entangle. The man generally is the active one and the woman the passive in a romantic encounter, although, as we shall soon see, both can be very manipulative.

Any romantic relationship between man and woman is obviously fertile ground for manipulation. (Curiously, people use the words "love" and "making love" for this activity.) Knowing, as we now do, that there is both active and passive manipulation, as well as active and passive actualization, it is time to make a clear distinction between actualizing and manipulating "love."

A man who is a manipulator sees every woman as an object, a sexual conquest, somebody to get something from. To him, women are things, not persons. The number of conquests he can boast of is his measure of manliness.

A woman manipulator uses men to make herself feel more attractive. She seeks out those men who will enhance her feelings of being sexually appealing. It isn't that she really desires the end result of sexual intercourse but rather that she likes the feeling of feminine appeal that the attention of men will give her. Often she's only a "teaser." An extremely manipulative woman derives great sadistic satisfaction from rejecting the man when he has committed his interests to her.

Let us now consider four situations in which manipulative love relationships occur.

EXAMPLE 1—*Jim and Jane.*

They meet at college and after several informal dates start "going together." Unfortunately, both Jim and Jane are manipulators and for these reasons:

1. *They are not honest.* Neither admits that he isn't truly interested in the other as a marriage mate. Instead, they play-act. Each deceives the other into thinking he is the "one and only," when it simply isn't true.

2. *It is a convenient relationship.* Neither Jim nor Jane needs to take the risk of seeking new friends as long as it is so convenient to have someone readily available. Neither, therefore, is *free.*

3. *Both are unaware* of, and unwilling to look at, the full limitations and potentialities of their relationship. Each is wasting important time of the other.

4. *Neither trusts* his own ability or the other's to enjoy a variety of friends on the open market.

EXAMPLE 2—Mary and Mac.

They meet at a cocktail party while their respective spouses are involved elsewhere. Mac suggests a rendezvous for lunch the following week, which they keep. After lunch and several martinis, Mac proposes that they go to a motel. Being an active manipulator, he doesn't like to waste time. Mary, however, is a passive manipulator and becomes indignant. She was enjoying the *pursuit.* The episode will be resolved either when she admits desire for him and goes to bed, or when he becomes aware that there is no hope for an easy conquest and bows out gracefully. A more persistent manipulator might continue to invest steaks and martinis in the pursuit.

Analysis.

In this situation each manipulator cares little for the personhood of the other. Neither is willing to take full responsibility for the consequences of an intimate relationship, and there is that risk in any relationship between two people. The manipulator wants to avoid that. One such risk may be an emotional involvement; another the actual risk of exposure. Mac desires a strictly sexual relationship that is easily controllable. Involvement could lead him to lose control, and the manipulator cannot bear to be without control of the situation.

Many men and women refuse to look at the business of an affair from a moral frame of references. Most do not respond to religious "shoulds" or "should nots." Ironically, however, when faced with the fact that they may only be manipulating, rather than really caring for the other person, they come to think seriously about the consequences of the affair.

EXAMPLE 3—Marvin.

He is furious with his wife. After they have fought all night, he promises himself: *I'll get even with her.* Arriving at the office next morning, he returns the smile of Millie, his secretary, with special warmth. Impulsively he invites her to join him for dinner. The game now is becoming more exciting. After several days of flirting, special attentions, and gifts, Millie is so overwhelmed that she agrees to meet Marvin for the night. Incidentally, Millie is not as innocent as he may think. She has been nurturing hidden thoughts of her own of how her boss's bed could be a launching pad for her career.

Analysis.

Marvin is elated and exhilarated over his affair with his secretary, not because he cares about her particularly but because she represents the means by which he can strike out at his wife. He derives great satisfaction from being able to deceive his wife, Martha. Rather than feeling affection for his lover then, he is using the affair as a means of expressing hostility toward his spouse. He may even say to Millie, in a manipulative gesture: "Give me time, darling, and I will leave my wife for you."

EXAMPLE 4—Martha.

Little though he may have known it, Marvin has left another manipulator waiting for him at home. How glad Martha is when she discovers the revealing note from Millie in her husband's pocket! Marvin, by his indiscretion, has martyred her, and he will pay for it. "How could you do this to me?" is her complaint, and it will echo in his ears for a long, long time. One thing is sure: no matter how he may plead, he'll get no divorce from her.

Analysis.

Rather than being truly unhappy or concerned or forgiving of her husband's indiscretion with another woman, Martha is thrilled to have found a club with which to bop him over the head. She will use this weapon against him until death do them part. Of course, Martha is safe from reproach, and whenever she pleases to use it, she has a tool for blackmailing Marvin into craven submission.

Let's retrace our steps and look at each of these four situations again, as it might have been if the parties involved were actualizors.

EXAMPLE 1—Jim and Jane.

Young lovers can be actualizing in their relationships if the following conditions attend:

150

1. *Each is honest.* Each is continuously open to expression of the changing feelings of both. When he, or she, sees the other as a potential marriage partner, he says so; when he does not, he doesn't deceive the other into thinking something that's not so. He doesn't play games with the other person as if she (or he) were a thing.

2. *If the relationship seems to lose value, each is willing to take the risk of terminating it.* Each is *free* and not controlled by a relationship that is dead.

3. *Both are aware of* the value and lack of value each has for the other. They continue to weigh one value against the other in a process of dynamic evaluation.

4. *Each trusts himself and the other* to cope with life. Manipulations or tricks, therefore, need not be used to keep the other person in line.

EXAMPLE 2—Mary and Mac.

Mac and Mary might also have related to each other in an actualizing way. Let us look back to the moment when they meet at the cocktail party. Each is attracted to the other, and their conversation might have gone like this:

Mac: I can't understand it, but I feel I want to see you again. There's something about you—something that's drawing me to you.

Mary: I guess I feel the same way. But it wouldn't be right—would it?

Mac: Well, that may be true, but my feelings tell me somehow that it would be right.

Mary: That bothers me, too. Do you often find that your feelings are contradictory to what society says you *should* do?

Mac: A lot of the time. But you know what? I've become patriotic to my own deepest feelings. I've got to see someone now, but I'm coming back before the night's over to ask you again. And I want an answer.

This would be an actualizing exchange in that each person is deeply honest in his expression. Mac, furthermore, is forceful in the expression of his feelings for Mary, though he is not trying to control her or manipulate her into a relationship which she doesn't really want. Finally, each is deeply aware of the conflict both are feeling inside, and each is willing to trust expressing these feelings to the other.

Once more we listen as they meet later in the evening:

Mac: Well, I'm back.

Mary: I was waiting for you.

Mac: Will you see me for lunch Wednesday?

Mary: Yes, I'll meet you at noon at Bailey's.

In this exchange, again, we see directness without decoercion. Mary openly admits her desire for his return. Neither is using the other; yet each, having been given time to think, still decides to risk an initial encounter.

Now the luncheon at Bailey's. After light conversation and an enjoyable lunch, they return to the deeper dialogue:

Mac: We're both married. You love your husband, and I love my wife. Yet we feel strongly attracted to each other. There are risks. Are we willing to face them?

Mary: I think I'm willing to take the risks, but I sense a reluctance on your part.

Mac: I guess you're right. Strange as it may seem, my caring for you says: "I'd rather love you and not hurt you than make love to you and hurt you."

It is obvious each has been thinking a great deal about the other. Mary is sensitive to the fact that Mac has developed some reservations and openly expresses her reaction. Mac doesn't deny his reservations in order to achieve his seduction but, rather, openly admits his caring could take a different direction.

EXAMPLE 3—*Marvin.*

We recall that Marvin, after a fight with his wife, has begun a flirtation with his secretary. Had each been dealing with the other in a more actualizing manner, their talk might have gone this way:

Millie: Gee. Mr. Miller, I have a feeling we're both on the wrong track. I have the deepest respect for you as an employer, and I also like Mrs. Miller.

Marvin: Oh hell! We're just getting going, and you have to mess it up by bringing her into it.

Millie: You have always seemed happy with your wife.

Marvin: It only appears that way. We put on a good front.

Millie: I guess that's what scares me—maybe you're just putting on a good front with me now.

Here, Millie is showing the kind of honesty that cares more for the other person's welfare than her own immedi-

ate satisfaction. An actualizor often will postpone immediate gratification for deeper values.

One of the major characteristics of an actualizing relationship is that feelings are carefully verbalized before
actions are expressed. Manipulators, by contrast, act impulsively without an awareness of their full range of
feelings and without any expression of the positives and
negatives which always exist within each of us.

EXAMPLE 4—Martha.

One of the most difficult problems in life is how to
react to the indiscretions of one's mate. The usual reaction is to blame, as Martha did on learning of her husband's affair. Karen Horney has dealt skillfully with this
issue in terms of the neurotic problems of the "innocent
party." She suggests that the major difficulty may not be
the infidelity, but the "innocent party's" *pride*.[1] When
Martha says, "How could you do this to me?" she really is
saying, "I am too great to have something like this happen
to me." This is her problem. What seems intolerable to
her is that her husband has slipped from her manipulative
control and domination. Not allowing him to get a divorce
is yet another form of control.

If Martha were an actualizor, she would have to admit
that things like this can happen to anyone, that she is only
a human being and has to examine ways in which she has
contributed to her husband's delinquency. In effect, he
shot the gun, but she helped load it. Further, she must
see how self-destructive would be her continued desire to
control her husband by not granting a divorce. Finally,
but most important, she will have to delve deep within
herself for the courage to forgive—which comes mighty
close to being divine.

Conclusions

In the game of "love," we see, it is very difficult to keep from being a manipulator. It is so easy always to regard the other person as a conquest rather than a person. The problems involved in these relationships, where each is indeed a live and quivering human being, must be dealt with on the feeling level without deception, without control. Most difficult of all is to be honest to *one's own feelings*. As these four not-uncommon situations indicate, however, it *is* possible.

The cases I have just described are real. They are typical of stories we hear in therapy daily. What conclusions can we draw from them?

It seems to me, first of all, that we must regard these as motivational problems, not as legalistic behavioral problems, i.e., right or wrong, and so forth. It is the inner attitude that counts, as Jesus said: "If thine eye be evil, thy whole body shall be full of darkness. If therefore the light that is in thee be darkness, how great *is* that darkness."

The issues in this chapter are best placed in the original formulations of manipulation vs. actualization. It is never actualizing to use or exploit another person, even if he is willing. The owner of a sweat shop may plead that his employees are eagerly grateful for the pittance he pays them as wages, but this does not render his abuse of them correct.[2] For the actualizor, love is not just an emotion or physical desire. It is concern and respect for the "thou" of the other. Treating another as a mere body makes the relationship an "it-it" one and not a "thou-thou" one. When sex is motivated by any need other than a "thou" form of caring, it becomes manipulative. For example, sex can be motivated by the anxiety of loneliness, the wish to conquer or be conquered, by vanity, or by the wish to hurt or even destroy.[3] When it is motivated by any of these rather than by love, the sexual act becomes manipulative, and this can happen either inside or outside a marriage relationship!

NOTES

1. Karen Horney, *Self-Analysis* (New York: W. W. Norton & Company, 1942), p. 283.
2. William G. Cole, *Sex in Christianity and Psychoanalysis* (New York: Oxford University Press, 1955), p. 26.
3. See *The Art of Loving*, p. 88.

CHAPTER 12

Teachers and Students

The classroom is a frighteningly fertile field for manipulation.

One major reason is the insistence by school administrators that above all else teachers maintain *control* over children. As we have seen, control of others, no matter how well-intentioned, reduces human beings to the status of things. In the classroom, too often, John and Mary, each of whom was born with the normal quota of human feelings, become units in a block of "pupils," the average daily attendance.

In this situation younger students particularly are challenged to counteract the controls. No doubt all of us will remember such "counter-actors" (teachers have called them "bad actors"), rebels, or class cutups from our own years in schoolrooms. We remember even their names, how they looked, and some of the techniques they used to combat teacher's control: giggling, grinning, asking irrelevant questions, passing notes, and so forth.

A teacher would have to be a genius to handle the multitudinous manipulations, or she must be a manipulator, too, and that, alas, is what many of our teachers are. Probably you remember your own teachers, both the good and the bad ones (only the names are changed), and the manipulative ways they controlled the "troublemakers": staring at the disruptive student; calling on him sharply by name; holding the offender for detention; sending home deficiency conduct notices; isolating him—standing him in the corner or moving his desk apart from other students; sending him to the office; using sarcasm and ridicule; making him sit in the front seat; creating guilt feelings, such as, "How can you do this to me when I only am trying to help you!"

The thing that is striking about these techniques is that they are all negative and controlling. They are directed toward the fostering of conformity rather than creativity. The pity of this is that, instead of encouraging inventiveness, innovation, and productivity, such manipulative behavior on the part of the teacher accomplishes just the reverse.

158

This is the paradox of the modern learning situation, and there is no simple solution for it. Pupils and teachers both are complex human beings living in the manipulative world of modern man. What we need most is a sensitivity to the fact that there is more to be done than we are doing.

Manipulative and Actualized Teaching

As long as we look at the problem strictly from the behavioral point of view, we miss something very vital. The alternative would be to look at it from the point of view of interest. It is well known that student interest in school decreases every year. What does this mean? Is it possible that school really is less interesting? Are outside activities so much more interesting than school? Are the teachers, perhaps, making learning less exciting? There is a good deal of evidence that this is exactly the point at which some teachers are failing and some of the youngsters with them.

Consider, if you will, some samples of classroom dialogue suggested by Richard Hogan [1] and decide for yourself which teachers are actualizing student interests and which are manipulating or controlling:

Ted: Teacher, would ants rather live inside than outside?

    Teacher A: I've never asked them. Let's stick to the lesson.

    Teacher B: I really don't know. Why don't you see whether more of them do stay inside than outside?

University student to professor: I've been thinking about the paper we must write for this class, and I wonder whether you'd prefer one on "Schools and Juvenile Delinquency" or one on "Intelligence of Criminals"?

Professor A:	Either would fit the requirement. I gather you're having trouble deciding which to work on.
Professor B:	I'd like you to do the one on "Intelligence of Criminals."

Mary: I'd like to put this design on the border of a play skirt for my little sister.

Teacher A:	Would you care to see if you could do some sewing in your crafts class?
Teacher B:	This is a class in art, not sewing.

Dan: Mr. Y, why isn't everybody double-jointed?

Teacher A:	We will take that up tomorrow. Today we are studying muscles.
Teacher B:	What did you wonder about it?

Marjorie: We have a cat that arches its back and hisses when we go near her babies.

Teacher A:	We don't care here how cats defend their young. We're talking about insects and birds and their protective coloration.
Teacher B:	You may see a relation between the protection of bugs by color and kittens by claws.

In each of the exchanges two teachers answer a student's question. In each case we see that the actualizing reply is the one that identifies and pursues valuable interests, even when they appear unrelated to the learning of the group or, perhaps, to the declared subject for that day. Manipulative comments are those that tell children their interests are unimportant or silly. As we know, it isn't going to be easy to change traditional classroom attitudes, but it would certainly seem that actualizing comments could reduce some of the myriad manipulations in education by creating interest and attention in the schoolroom.

Many, many teachers feel they are actualizing in their approach to their classrooms, but I would still like to make some suggestions relative to student "questions." [2]

1. *Take time to understand a question.* In discussion, it is not unusual, during the interval in which we aren't speaking, to think of what we will say next, rather than to listen to what others are saying. The discussion thus becomes "parallel monologues" rather than a dialogue. In teaching, this tendency leads to a lecture addressed to a question that hasn't really been asked. (I know this because I have taught.) However exhilarated it may make teachers feel, the student is left feeling misunderstood. Rephrasing the question may help student and teacher understand each other. Asking for a repetition of the question or simply admitting, "Sorry, I didn't understand," may show respect for the learner, and he senses this.

2. *A question often deserves more than an answer.* There is a strange theory prevalent in our expert-ridden society that a question deserves only an exact answer. The assumption then is that when an answer is given, the recip-

ient immediately knows what the answerer has meant. Semanticists call this the fallacy of "perfect communication." The fact is that each of us tends to place greatest trust in our own common sense—that which we have learned for ourselves. This is true of the learner. An opportunity to grapple with a problem and work it out produces meaningful learning. A hasty answer often limits the learning possible in the area questioned.

3. *Answering too readily may hasten the tendency to rely on outside experience rather than to look within.* To "look to the expert" is appropriate in certain technical fields, but perhaps the real reason students stop thinking at such a young age is that, when they have questions, they have discovered it is easier to ask someone who knows. Becoming satisfied with the answers of others, they learn not to rely on their own techniques of problem solving. Undoubtedly it is gratifying to reveal our uncommon wisdom to the apparently eager listener. Nevertheless, a too pat answer may seriously dam up an area of the learner's development and stultify his tendency to be self-directive.

4. *Questions may mean something other than answer-seeking.* A young student once asked a teacher: "What makes thunder?" After the teacher had answered with an explanation of the dynamics of electric storms, the student asserted: "That's not right; my father says a tractor makes thunder." Very little can be done in such a situation as this although it might have been avoided if the teacher had asked simply after the original question, "What makes you ask?" In a sense, the youngster's question probably meant, "I've heard something that's interesting." If the

teacher had given him a chance to express what he was thinking, he would have had a chance to contribute something to the group and perhaps pursue his interests in tractors and in thunder. Questions like this often are actually openings for a comment and not searchings for an answer.

Sometimes questions are contrived more to get the lay of the land than an answer. A student with guilt feelings about obedience might ask: "Do you think a child has to obey his mother all the time?" It would be extremely difficult for a teacher to know what such a question really does mean, of course. Most likely the child is not interested in the ethics of the problem but is testing to see how teacher will react so he will know if it's safe to continue. An answer here has interesting possibilities. If the teacher says, "Yes, a child should obey at all times," the discussion is likely to become academic since the youngster now feels it isn't safe to reveal his misbehavior. If the teacher says, "No," the child might then feel that what he has done is justified and may not explore the implications of his deed. A third and better answer, remaining interested but noncommittal, might be the simple statement: "You're wondering about having to obey." Thus, she frees the atmosphere for a full expression of the child's concern.

In the broad sense, all questions represent growth pains in self-development, and with careful cultivation the youngster may be helped to grow. Appropriate self-restraint on the part of the teacher helps self-development in the child. Understanding, respecting, and encouraging the child's questions actualize his budding interests. Manipulative answers which slam the door on him, in the name of control, shut off dialogue, stifle interest, and stunt growth.

Teen-Ager/Teacher Relationships

The teen-ager is a special problem in education very often because of compulsory school attendance. Edgar Friedenberg has stated that a school must regulate behavior that would interfere with instruction, and compulsory school attendance gives schools the force of law.[3] They are empowered, for example, to censor school newspapers, ban controversial speakers, supervise associations, enforce regulations on dress and grooming, and so forth. What does this make of the teacher and principal but parent substitutes? Are they *valid* substitutes? How could they possibly be?

Friedenberg goes on to say that the teen-ager doesn't really rebel against teachers but is only disillusioned or indifferent. This action is different from that which he takes toward his parents, toward whom he rebels more actively. Labeling the teen-ager a rebel is assuming that he believes the authority he is fighting is legitimate, even though objectionable. The more disaffected of our youth intend no such compliment. Their attitude toward school and teachers is like disenchanted Alice in Wonderland, who exclaims to the deranged and pretentious creatures who had previously intimidated her: "Why, you're only a pack of cards, anyway!" [4] That the teen-ager is indifferent or disillusioned is illustrated by his constant rejoinder: "So what's the big deal?" Our adolescents are so reality-oriented in their peer groups that education is no longer a revelation.

Teen-agers may also become disillusioned because, so

often, they feel their teachers have little respect for them. Remember that to some teachers, youth is defined as something of a half-adult which needs supervision to keep from getting into trouble, and generally the adolescent takes to the road of passive manipulation. If the teacher gives him the name, he may play the game of passivity and indifference. Perhaps some teachers need to consider the comments made by teen-agers to one school counselor:

"Teachers are phoney. They say they are concerned about us, but they just want us to make them look good. They're concerned with our behavior as it reflects on their teaching, and they don't really care about us."

Hustling: The Students' Manipulation

Responding to teachers, as his concept of them suggests, the student becomes a "hustler." He resorts to underhanded con games to manipulate older people. Some forms of hustling used in schools today would be:

1. *Playing the home against the teacher.* "My mother says this assignment is silly." "I couldn't do my homework because we had company last night." "My father doesn't believe this."

2. *Helplessness.* "I can't do it; help me."

3. *Sickness.* Going to the nurse's office frequently, especially when there are tests.

4. *Seduction.* "I've just got to get a 'B' in order to get into college." "You're the best teacher I ever had."

5. *Playing one teacher against the other.* "We have fun in Mr. Edwards' class."

6. *Putting the cat on teacher's back.* "I could learn English if it just were made more interesting."

Manipulations of the Teacher

Teacher is not without guilt either. Since schooltime began, she used little tricks to control young people:

1. *Using the spy system.* Vice-principals may use children to spy on each other for smoking, swearing, and such.

2. *Using the pet system.* Special students are made favorites, given the errands to run, "good conduct rewards."

3. *Suspending.* Difficult teen-agers are suspended, jeopardizing graduation, or this is threatened constantly.

4. *Embarrassing.* Difficult children "pay" for their sins by being made a fool of and ridiculed before their friends.

5. *Using grades to punish.* Punishing a child with a "C" to keep him off the honor roll; punishing with "unsatisfactory conduct" marks to make him ineligible for athletic teams or clubs. (Grades control parents, too.) A "C" instead of a "B" can keep a child off the honor roll. An "F" instead of a "D" keeps him from graduating.

6. *Comparing unfavorably.* Comparing a child's work negatively with previous work of an older sibling. One of the most obstreperous teen-agers any school ever had to work with got that way, in part, because in the lower grades he followed a straight "A" sister who was to go on and earn her Ph.D. in mathematics. The boy's interests were totally different from hers, but teachers invariably chided him with remarks like: "Why can't you be like your sister?" The poor kid had to rebel to preserve his identity.

Actualizing Students' Learning

At the beginning of this discussion we noted that conformity and active control are values that the average teacher exerts in dealing with the manipulation of students. It is paradoxical, then, that creative or actualizing students, as research shows, have the following characteristics: a reputation for having wild, silly, and "naughty" ideas; a tendency to produce ideas "off the beaten track"; a tendency to produce work characterized by humor, playfulness, lack of rigidity, and relaxation.[5] In general, they are not easily "molded" or controlled, and maybe that's why the "crazy kid" we remember from school went on to make his creative mark in life. It was a struggle, but he managed somehow to overcome the stultifying, repressive manipulations of a series of mediocre teachers.

Teaching which would help students actualize would be teaching which centers on the *interests* of student and teacher; encourages full expression of feelings and ideas of students; handles student questions and asks questions, skillfully; allows full expression of the teachers' ideas and feelings as well.

To weary teachers who would tell us they have enough to do in their over-crowded schedules without getting involved in theories of "manipulation" and "actualizing," I would reply: A new breed of teacher is coming, and she will be a good one. I think of Joan, who is twenty-eight and has, with the help of her principal and a sensitivity training group, become actualizing with her students. She says of it:

I had a great feeling of relief when I began to understand that a youngster needs more than just subject matter. Oh, I know mathematics well, and I teach it well. I used to think that that was all I needed to do. Now I teach children, not math. I accept the fact that I can succeed only partially with some of them. I have found further that *my own personhood*

167

has educatable value. When I don't have to know all the answers, I seem to have more answers than before when I tried so hard to be the expert. The youngster who really made me understand this was Eddie. I asked him one day why he thought he was doing so much better than last year. He gave meaning to my whole new orientation. "It's because I like myself now when I'm with you," he said.

NOTES

1. From an unpublished manuscript, "Psychology of the Learning Process."

2. *Ibid.*

3. See "A Ministry in Need of New Rights," p. 85 in *The Young Americans.*

4. *Ibid.,* p. 86.

5. Ellis P. Torrance, *Guiding Creative Talent* (Englewood Cliffs, N. J.: Prentice-Hall, 1962).

CHAPTER 13

Husbands and Wives

Ambrose Bierce, in his sardonic way, defined marriage as "a community consisting of a master, a mistress, and two slaves, making in all, two." Ibsen spoke of it as "a thing you've got to give your whole mind to," and Tennyson theorized that marriages are made in heaven. Most married men will agree, however, that marriages are very much something that must be lived here on earth, and we all have our ideas as to how that is to be done.

No doubt you have your views on marriage, and this is a good time to see what they are. Therefore we open this chapter with a "Marriage Quiz." Answer each of the seventeen statements with a *T* for True or *F* for False. The right answers will be found at the end of the chapter, but don't look now. Take the test and see how you feel about marriage; then read the psychologist's ideas, and maybe you'll wish to change some answers before you grade yourself.

____1. Love is a singular feeling which you either feel or not toward another person.

____2. It is unwise to be childlike in a marriage relationship.

____3. Lovers can't be friends.

____4. Jealousy is a dangerous thing in a marriage.

____5. Marriage is a fusion of two people who become "one."

____6. The best way to love in a marriage is to subordinate your own needs to your partner's.

____7. A wife should realize that her husband has a form of "ownership" of her if she is married to him.

____8. Married partners should allow the other partner to use or exploit them when necessary.

____9. A wife should give herself sexually to her husband whenever he demands it.

____10. Anger is the opposite of love; therefore, a loving relationship should not ever be an angry one.

____11. Criticism is better than getting angry.

_____12. Feelings need reasons to justify them.

_____13. Hurting another person's feelings in a marriage conflict should be avoided at all costs.

_____14. Marital fights are really unnecessary if the people are smart enough to reason out the issues.

_____15. People should have control over their emotions and not "lose control" and yell and scream.

_____16. Crying is something to be avoided in a marriage relationship.

_____17. People who really love each other don't have to fight. Love conquers all.

Married people live in a legal relationship of intimacy. In any relationship this close, the strongest feelings will have to be dealt with, and the strongest of all feelings are love and hate.

Manipulative vs. Actualizing Love

Love has several forms. Let's see how each may be used in marriage.

1. *Affection.* This is an unconditional caring or affection such as a parent has for a child. The danger is that parents sometimes begin to feel they "own" their child, and then affection turns into owning. The same principle holds in marriage. One marriage partner never really *owns* the other. Even marriage vows have been changed with this in mind. Once they required the parties to "love and *obey.*" Now it is "love *cherish.*" An actualizing marriage relationship is one in which there is appreciation and valuing of the other's "thou-ness," never regarding her, or him, manipulatively as a *thing* or an *it.* Manipulative affection

171

is that in which the husband feels he owns his wife to the point that at parties he can't be comfortable sharing her, even in conversation, with other men.

2. *Friendship*. Being a love of equals, friendship is based on an appreciation of the other person's principal talents and worth. Friendship may become manipulative, however, when we begin to "exploit" or use another person rather than to appreciate him. An example of friendship which turns into exploitation is one in which an individual, perhaps without realizing what he is doing, continually asks for favors which require much time and effort. True friendship requires respect for the other person's time and personhood.

3. *Eros*. Eros is a romantic love, which includes inquisitiveness, jealousy, and exclusiveness, as well as sexual desire. Romantic, sexual love easily becomes manipulative, and we refer to it as "seduction." Seduction is using the other person's body physically, without appreciating her total spiritual nature. An example of seduction (or adultery inside a marriage) is a husband's using his wife physically without regard for her personal feelings.

4. *Empathy*. A charitable, altruistic form of love, which cares deeply for the other person as a unique human being, empathy sometimes is called charity or compassion. When we empathize manipulatively, we use the feelings of ourselves or another to *control* him, rather than to understand him. For example, we may empathically sense that our spouse has just punished a child in order to get the upper hand in an argument, and now feels guilty about doing so. Instead of understanding the guilt with a comment such as, "I know you feel bad," we can use the

knowledge that he feels guilty and rub it in deeper with a comment like, "You really feel you goofed."

5. *Self-Love.* Self-love is the ability to accept one's strengths, as well as one's weaknesses. Self-love becomes manipulative when a person treats the *self* as an object or thing, rather than someone to be respected. In the sexual realm we call this prostitution, the giving away of one's body without respect for it. To allow oneself to be used by other people is a form of prostitution. In marriage, for example, one is prostituting oneself when he allows his spouse to take advantage of his talents without setting any limits. To love oneself is to appreciate one's limits and to say "No" when one cannot give freely.

"B" vs. "D" Love

Abraham Maslow makes a distinction between "B" love and "D" love.[1] B love stands for *being* love, and D for *deficiency* love. When we love another in a B way, we love him in an admiring, respectful way. We love him as an end in himself; we love him for his "is-ness." When we love in a D way, however, we exploit and manipulate the other person. We love him as a means rather than as an end. We "should" him rather than accepting him as he is. Maslow gives this example from the pet world: Dog "improvers" are D lovers with all their tail cropping, ear cropping, and selective breeding since these meet needs of the trainer, not the dog. Real dog lovers are B lovers because they like the little old mutt just as he is, happy and wagging.

The B lover is not interfering and demanding, but can delight in the other person as he is. The D lover is more like a butcher, a sculptor modeling clay, or a conquerer demanding unconditional surrender. In marriage, we love in some combination of B and D. B love, beyond a shadow of a doubt, is a richer, higher, more valuable love than D love. The manipulative person loves with greater D and less B. The actualizing person, however, loves with greater B and some D. Research on the *Caring Relationship Inventory* [2] has shown that actualizing couples love in a B/D ratio of about two to one.

Anger and Hatred

We usually think of anger and hatred as being the opposite of love. In a marriage relationship the problem of aggression is a continuous one. For this reason I would like to suggest some clearer meanings for these terms.

1. *Hostility.* Hostility is negative and destructive. It is not a feeling, but an attitude which makes no contact with the other person. Hostility is expressed in the marriage by dirty looks and the "silent treatment" or sarcasm. It is hardly conducive to good contact.

2. *Anger.* Anger is a valuable feeling and an assertive method of making contact. Perls has said that anger is a sympathetic feeling. It unites people because it is mixed with caring. The goal of anger is not to destroy a relationship but to break down the barrier which is blocking contact with the other person. To be angry from time to time is to love and desire contact with the other. Without anger, love stagnates and becomes contactless. For instance, "You really make me mad when you won't talk to me," says the husband in a moment of loving candor.

3. *Resentment.* This is a hostile demand for the other person to feel guilty. Examples: "I can't understand why dinner isn't ready when I get home." Or, "If you really

loved me, you wouldn't want to play golf without me every weekend."

4. *Guilt.* Guilt usually is defined as a negative feeling toward oneself for having done something wrong. The paradoxical fact is that the more a person feels saintly, the more he experiences guilt; the more knowledge of wrong you have, the more you are aware of ways to do wrong. The resentment underlying guilt is related to *not* doing instead of to doing. The resentment is that others can do it, but the saint cannot. Perls believes that ninety percent of guilt is really, deep down, hostility toward others and therefore, is phoney rather than authentic guilt. Granted, some guilt is genuine, and when one can truly accept responsibility for certain undesired outcomes, guilt can be authentic. But much "guilt" is more of the following order: *"I* should not have done it" can be translated into *"You* should not have done it." *"I* feel so guilty that I didn't do it" can be translated into "I feel resentful that *you* didn't do it." To illustrate:

"I hate myself when I act like this." (Guilt feeling.) Turning the guilt into hostility, it can be translated into "I resent *you* for doing this when I cannot." Another translation would be: "I resent *you* when you act like this."

We may conclude that much guilt feeling is really hostility or hypocrisy rather than genuine guilt and that the expression of guilt is often really an indirect attempt to criticize others. Thus, the expression of guilt may be seen as a manipulation, inflicting hostility inward that really should be expressed outwardly.

5. *Hurt.* Perls says that ninety percent of hurt is vindictiveness. Therefore, when one says, "I feel so hurt,"

he often feels no hurt at all, but revenge. The wife who says she is hurt when her husband forgets her anniversary isn't really hurt, but angry at him for having forgotten. This does not mean that all hurt is vindictiveness because sometimes we do feel genuinely sad and tearful. Nevertheless, we should be careful to examine our hurt and see whether or not it may be vindictiveness. For instance, Wife: "I feel so hurt when you don't seem ever to care about anyone in my family." Translated, it often means: "I'm sore because you don't like my family."

A marriage relationship that contains no hurt is a mutual protection society or a hothouse relationship. Hurting is a necessary part of a healthy relationship. As we have pointed out earlier, the deepest faith that can exist between a husband and a wife is that the other person can take what we have to offer at the feeling level. If we can disengage ourselves from the need to win in a marriage conflict, then conflict becomes a fertile field in which solutions can come. If a loved one dies, for example, it is important to feel the hurt or engage in grief or mourning so that unfulfilled desires and impossible hopes can be relinquished. Once the mourning is over, new interests are possible. Further, emotional pain and hurt, when expressed and felt deeply, lead to strength and growth. Marriage isn't, and should not be, a mutual protection society. Hurt, of course, brings crying and tears, which need to be expressed like any other feeling, and hurting often leads to a counterattack by the other spouse. We need to recognize that attacks often come when another is hurt deeply. Understanding this is most important. Example:

Wife: I'm really getting fed up—you just don't give me enough money to run this house.

Husband: Your voice sounds to me as though it has more hurt in it than anger.

Wife: Yes, I am deeply hurt that I don't have enough money to dress decently.

Here is illustrated the importance of recognizing hurt in the voice of the sender when she may only be aware of anger.

6. *Hatred.* Hatred is hostility which has become set and is self-destructive. To hate someone is binding energy and, therefore, is economically wasteful. Hatred should be turned into contactful anger. Hatred not expressed can create sickness in the hater.

7. *Criticalness.* Criticalness is negativity with or without feeling. Psychologically it can be cowardly since there is no release of emotion. It then becomes manipulative because it attacks the other person in a "needling" way, without feeling. Criticalness which is allowed to be expressed *with feeling* creates contact. Criticalness which does not express feeling simply creates resentment. In a marriage criticalness on the part of the wife usually is referred to as "bitching," which means picking at little things without any real feeling about what is really bothering her. More often than not, it is a form of displacement. A suggestion for avoiding criticalness would be to change it into honest anger, which then recreates contact. For example, the wife says, "You are home late again. Dinner is going to be late. Jimmy has been bad all day. And would you look at the washing machine? I think it's broken again." On reexamination, her comments might conceivably be turned into genuine anger, such as, "I'm still mad at you for not taking me to the party last week!"

177

8. *Withdrawal.* One may withdraw from a contact relationship, either physically or by pouting or being silent. As we have said earlier, withdrawal from contact over a prolonged period may be wise, but often withdrawal from contact at the peak of a marital conflict is a way of controlling and keeping the situation from being terminated. Fights are not concluded by premature withdrawal, such as the husband walking off at the height of the conflict, saying: "I can't talk to you." This situation is unfinished, both parties feel *incomplete.*

9. *Indifference.* By indifference, we mean having no feeling, either positive or negative, toward the other person. This is a serious situation since indifference is the absence of caring and is most detrimental in a marriage relationship. As long as there is hostility or hatefulness and especially anger, feelings still exist toward the other person, and the relationship is not dead. When there is indifference only, a relationship is dead.

The Importance of Conflict

In marriage, conflict is seen as negative feelings between two people arising out of differing needs or goals. We are suggesting that conflict is not bad but necessary and that there can be creative conflict. Conflict requires expression of *feelings,* not just logic. Feelings need to be expressed deeply and do not need reasons for expression. Out of conflict a couple can grow together. In this attitude there also is involved an attitude of faith—faith that each will prove adequate to the resolution of the conflict. In creative conflict the warring of marital partners can lead to creative solutions. The actualizing married partner respects differences in his spouse just as the creative scientist looks for disproving evidence. Indeed, the actualizing marriage partner is grateful for conflict.

Marital Fighting

The healthy marriage is one in which creative fighting and conflict more often are present than not. It is a working relationship for conflict and resultant growth. Love doesn't mean not fighting. Good heavens, no! People who love each other and are close need to fight once in a while. Many people have come mistakenly to fear expression of strong feelings in the marriage relationship, assuming that they should be rational and logical, which means trying to convince each other by facts rather than by expressing their feelings. The real fear of expressing anger or disagreement, however, is a fear of being hurt, or a fear of feeling guilt for inflicting hurt, or even fear of abandonment. This fear causes people to deny their natural hostile feelings with the result that they experience guilt, nag about unimportant things, or develop psychosomatic complaints. (They actually get sick!) A marital fight involves the expression of strong feelings, and strong feelings need to be regarded as normal from time to time.

Here is an example of argument conducted in a manipulative way:

Wife: I suppose you'll be gone again this weekend. (She is making a predictive assumption.)

Husband: And I suppose you're going to gripe as usual.

Wife: Well, I'm about ready to give up. We don't have any marriage at all.

Husband:	I agree. I don't see why we've stayed married this long.
Wife:	You don't ever appreciate how lonesome I am and how much trouble it is being with the kids all the time. (Now she is demanding appreciation.)
Husband:	And you don't appreciate how hard I work to keep you in this expensive house and pay for every damned thing you buy.
Wife:	OK. So I'll go out and work. You can take care of the kids. Or we'll find someone to take care of them.
Husband:	Hell, you don't know how to do anything. You couldn't make any money, anyway. By the time we got through paying taxes we'd be deeper in the hole. (He is depreciating his partner's worth.)

The purpose of an argument should never be to win, but to express one's whole self in the conflict. Actualizing family discussions do not have to be friendly. What, then, is the alternative? We offer some suggestions for handling your feelings in an actualizing way:

1. *Become aware of bipolarity in an argument.* By this we mean, of course, that there always are two reasonable points of view being expressed in the argument, and both points of view really exist inside ourselves and the other person. One way to become aware of the bipolarity in an argument is to present your own point of view as openly as possible and then listen for your partner's point of view. Try then to repeat what the other has said before continuing. For example:

Husband: Dammit, I know you're upset because I'm going this weekend. But there's just no other way.

Wife: But that's the way it is every weekend. You can always find something to do besides stay home with me and the children. I get lonesome.

Husband: I know you feel upset and lonely, and it does seem I'm gone every weekend.

Wife: And I realize you've got to be gone a lot if we want the business to do well.

In this interchange, both husband and wife express negative feelings, after which the internal teeter-totter in the husband shifts. He is then able to verbalize his wife's viewpoint, which actually is the opposite of his own (but is *within himself* on that teeter-totter). This leads the wife to do the same. The natural organismic balance begins to work in both, and the conflict may be resolved.

2. *Give evidence to support your viewpoint and express your feelings as directly as possible.* Do not let fear of emotions prevent you from expressing them.

Wife: I know you love me, but darn it, you really don't know how bored I get. Two weeks ago you were gone four nights, plus the weekend, and this week you're gone three nights, plus the weekend.

Husband: But you don't appreciate why. Last month we were $900 in the red, and this month we're going to be $500 in the black because

I've been taking time to go out and get the business.

Here, both are giving data to support their points of view. Neither is fearful of expressing his feelings along with the data.

3. *Entertain differences.* Seriously entertain the other person's ideas; try them for fit, work them over, work yourself over. In this way you can know how much to accept, reject, partly accept, or partly reject. Welcome the opportunity to extend your knowledge or replace an outworn assumption.

Wife: I appreciate the money, and I do notice the difference this month. But can't we limit the time you're away from home and still be in the black?

Husband: OK. I think I can do it by staying out only two nights a week and an occasional weekend. We're over the hump now anyway.

Here, as a result of expression, progress is being made.

4. *Appreciate differences.* Recognize that another's opinions, tastes, and responsibilities must be respected. Welcome the excitement and growth that come from any difference.

Wife: Anyway, I'm glad I mentioned it. Nothing would have changed if I hadn't.

This shows the value of the expression of conflict.

5. *After hearing each other out with rebuttals and counter rebuttals, keep talking until each feels better.*

Failure to express feelings, as well as ideas, verbally leads to force, brutality, escapism, and other forms of open marital discord. It is better to scream and yell if the tension is within, to give feelings a release. "Letting go" of control is consciously letting go of feelings deeply felt and is different from "losing control."

Husband: Well, I'm glad you complained. I feel better toward you now.

When enough of the dirty water gets out, there's room for clean water.

6. *Always leave plenty of time for a family discussion.* Handling feelings takes time. "Never let the sun set on your wrath."

Wife: Now we can both go to bed and sleep.

Feelings not expressed cause internal tension and conflict. A good, finished argument is better than a sleeping pill.

Some Conclusions

If we can believe that our feelings are natural and worthwhile expressions of our developing selfhood, then we can learn to express *all* of them—the negative, hostile ones as well as the positive. When negative feelings are expressed, other positive ones can then be allowed into consciousness. This leads to the view that expression of our negative, hurtful feelings is necessary for an actualizing marital relationship. When one partner feels hostile toward the other, such feelings may often represent an active desire for the other to realize more of his potential. This is an expression of true caring. The desire to com-

183

municate and be close can transcend the fear of being hurt in return.

It is possible to manipulate the spouse by appealing to his sense of vanity, ego, self-esteem, or good judgment, but such mental trickery is easily found out and resented. Life cannot be a masquerade.

A respect for your spouse's "righteous indignation" and his right to express it, even if you do not agree, is the foundation of a healthy marriage. A happy marriage is a workshop for growth, and a workshop needs conflict and fighting. Each person grows from each battle with a worthy foe.

Here I offer a summary of destructive and constructive fight styles.

Destructive Fight Styles

1. Apologizing prematurely.

2. Refusing to take the fight seriously.

3. Withdrawing; evading "toe-to-toe confrontation"; walking out; falling asleep; applying the "silent treatment."

4. Using intimate knowledge of partner to hit "below the belt," playing the Humiliator.

5. Chain-reacting—throwing in the kitchen sink from left field, bringing in unrelated issues to pyramid the attack.

6. Being a "pseudo-accommodator"—pretending to go along with partner's point of view for momentary peace, but hoarding doubts, secret contempt, resentments, private reservations.

7. Attacking indirectly (against some person, idea,

activity, value, or object which the partner loves or stands for) —"Carom fighting."

8. Being a "double binder"—setting up expectations but making no attempt to fulfill them; giving a rebuke instead of a reward.

9. "Character analysis"—explaining what the other person's feelings are.

10. Demanding more—"Gimme"—nothing is ever enough.

11. Withholding—affection, approval, recognition, material things, privileges—anything which would give pleasure or make life easier for the partner.

12. Undermining—deliberately arousing or intensifying emotional insecurities, anxiety, or depression; keeping partner on edge; threatening disaster.

13. Being a "Benedict Arnold"—not only failing to defend the partner, but encouraging attacks from outsiders.

Constructive Fight Styles

1. Program fights at special times to avoid wear and tear on innocent bystanders. Leave plenty of time to handle feelings.

2. Each partner gives full expression to his own positive feelings.

3. Each partner gives full expression to his own negative feelings.

4. Each one replays partner's argument in his *own* words, to be sure he understands it.

5. Entertain the "feedback" of the other person's

evaluation of your behavior. This means "chewing over" evaluations of yourself before accepting or rejecting them.

6. Define clearly what the fight is about.

7. Discover where the two positions coincide as well as differ.

8. Each partner defines his "out-of-bounds" areas of vulnerability.

9. Determine how deeply each partner feels about his stake in the fight. This enables each to decide how much he can yield.

10. Offer correctional critiques of conduct—this means for both to develop positive suggestions for improvement in each other.

11. Decide how each can help the other relative to the problem.

12. Recognize the Yablonsky (spontaneous explosion without reason) and wait for it to subside; don't "hook in."

13. Try to score the fight by comparing the learning yield of the fight against the injury. Winners are those who learn more than they get hurt.

14. Fight—after thinking. Compare your opinions with each other after the leftovers, evasions, and unsettled issues, if any.

15. Declare a fight holiday, a truce, a period of time in which no fight engagements are to be made. This provides the conditions for exercising the fine art of making up and enjoying its benefits, such as warm body contact, good sex, etc.

16. Be prepared for the next fight. Intimate fighting is more or less continuous, and paradoxically if it is accepted and expected, the quality of fighting is less vicious, the fights less long, the injury less, and the learning of new aspects more.[3]

I recognize that different partners in a marriage have different backgrounds, different expectancies, different patterns regarding expressing feelings of anger, acceptability of anger, and so forth. Therefore, there may be a need for time and patience until they get to the point where they can fight well. This chapter is not a prescription for what a couple should immediately try to do. It is a description of what can be aimed toward. So how did you do on the Marriage Quiz? The answers to all the questions are "False."

NOTES

1. See *Toward a Psychology of Being.*
2. E. L. Shostrom, *Caring Relationship Inventory.* San Diego: Educational and Industrial Testing Service, 1966.
3. The destructive and constructive fight styles presented here were developed by Dr. George R. Bach of Beverly Hills, California. They are here adapted from an article about Dr. Bach's work in *Life* magazine ("The Marital Fight Game") of May 17, 1963.

CHAPTER 14

Profit vs. Persons

I notice all through these pages that my case histories show businessmen coming to me for help in their personal lives. The paradox is that they are very successful men, according to their profit and loss statements, yet seem to be most unsuccessful measured by the quality of their interpersonal relationships. They can't seem to avoid problems with their wives or their children or their friends. Obviously the question arises: is the underlying philosophy of business a breeder of manipulators?

This has to concern us because the most potent single institution in our American culture is business and industry, and there are some critics who suggest that many American industrial leaders have used manipulation to achieve their goals. As we have seen throughout this book, manipulation in *personal* relations is dangerous and self-defeating. But maybe the rules for business and personal life are different? In business a person has to make a profit, and that might seem to require manipulation.

In an area as big and complex as this, I do not pretend to give hard-and-fast answers. I go back instead to the basic principle on which the book is based. You will remember that I referred to the manipulative relationship as an "It-It" relationship in which the person who regards another as an "it" or a "thing" also becomes an "it" or "thing." A businessman who thinks of people only as customers or accounts or clients cannot help, to some degree, regarding these persons as things. When profit is the primary concern, then, it seems to me from my own experience that it is easy to lose one's sensitivity to the personhood of another.

Earlier, I proposed that the model for an actualizing relationship is a "Thou-Thou" relationship, where the person who regards another as a "thou" also becomes a "thou." In my work as therapist, this is easy for me to do since therapy is based on respect for the dignity and worth of one's client. But the fact that he *is* a client, and not just a person, makes him also a matter of financial concern to me. When I am being the businessman, rather than the psychologist, it is difficult not to let the "thou" become a "thing."

Perhaps people don't think of the psychologist in terms of his being also a businessman. Make no mistake about it, though, I must be a businessman and must, therefore, have this great general conflict in myself. At the Institute, for instance, I have a sizeable overhead to be met every month before I can start earning a livelihood for my family. I must charge a fee for my services and must collect my accounts. An electric typewriter costs me just as much as it does General Motors. I have gas bills, electrical bills, a huge telephone bill, and must buy malpractice insurance the same as doctors and lawyers. I pay five cents to mail a letter or the bill for my services just as the businessman down the street does. I must pay Social Security and with-holding taxes on the skilled secretaries who have typed these words. The conflict between the businessman side of me and the therapist side of me is ever present.

I would like to propose that there is an interesting parallel between my work as psychologist and that of the businessman. To the therapist, the patient is relatively the same as the employee or customer is to the businessman; the patient who comes to the institute is both a person to be helped and a client to be served. To the businessman, although he may not always remember it, his customer and employees are as much persons as are his wife and children.

The basic problem of the patient is that he uses "crutches" when he doesn't need them. He tries constantly to manipulate the therapist for support, and my job is to frustrate him in his demands so he can stop manipulating and become self-actualizing—so he can trust himself rather than depend on me or other people. The less internal support he has, the more he has to manipulate.

A parallel situation exists between employee and employer. The employee is a person who depends on his employer for economic support. In an age of fringe benefits it is only natural that he will try to get as many as he can for as little work as possible. In this he is like the patient trying to get as much support from the psychologist as the traffic will bear. An actualizing employer would be the one who helps his employee become increasingly self-supporting, in the sense that he learns to do the job better. But then, ironically, the employee may want more of the profit or more rewards for doing his job better, and the facts of good business practice are that there is a limit to how much you can pay him. We are seeing the ultimate tragedy of this on all sides of our modern society in the growth of automation. Here the employer, of necessity, is learning to make *things*—machines—replace people.

There is another parallel. A patient sometimes demands excessive attention at all hours of the day or night, whenever he is in trouble and thinks I should help; he also feels entitled to run up as large a bill as he needs. Some even expect me to see them for nothing if they are unable to pay, manipulating me into thinking I am a public servant who cannot deny the needy. The answer to them must be: My love is free, but you must pay for my time. I will continue to regard the individual as a "thou," but my time is limited, and I must be recompensed for it.

The businessman has a similar implied philosophy toward his customers. His attitude, for instance: You expect of me certain services; you expect conveniences from my place of business, savings, quality, personal attention. The bargain-conscious customer, on his part, demands that the businessman charge less than his competition. (As witness to this, we have the current mushroom growth of discount houses.) The facts of economic life are that the merchant expects to provide products as cheaply as it can be done but expects also that you, the customer, pay for the services rendered.

At this point advertising complicates the problem. In order to attract the customer to a given merchant or product, advertising attempts to portray that store or that commodity as the best or the cheapest, whether it always is true or not. Advertising costs money, of course, and that must be added to the price of the product. Consider the phenomenon of trading stamps. We are led to assume that the stamps are given to us free with our purchases and that we may obtain expensive articles for them gratis. In reality, of course, we pay for these bonus items because they have been paid for by the retailer, who has added the expense of the stamps to the cost of the product he sold us in the first place. We allow ourselves to be manipulated in this stamp dealing, pleasant though it may seem.

Selling intrudes a further complication in this matter of profit versus persons. To sell we must have salesmen, and again it is Abraham Maslow who offers us some thinking.[1] The typical salesman is profit motivated. He knows he must curry favor with the customer by building his loyalty; therefore, the salesman is prepared to spend substantial amounts of expense money entertaining customers and cementing their friendship to induce purchasing. He is the manipulator par excellence. I have, as a matter of fact, had a number of salesmen as patients who had to give up the work because they were becoming ill from having to play phony friendship games with people they didn't really like. The usual salesman, as we would expect, is a profit-oriented man, loyal to his company and product, who functions partially on a selective presentation of information and truth. The main goal of his business dealings is to market the product (even though it may be inferior) since the success of his company depends on it.

Maslow suggests an alternative. He suggests that businessmen try to assume that the good customer is a rational human being who prefers quality in merchandising, that he has taste and is capable of righteous indignation. This customer realizes that expense account lunches and phony friendship weekends are actually costs which will only be added to the price of the product. Maslow proposes then that the salesman re-identify himself as a man of integrity who knows his product and the market, sees himself as an "ambassador" in the business world, relying upon honesty, truthfulness, and full disclosure of the facts. To this type of salesman, *marketing of the product would be secondary to the interests and needs of the customer*. This might even mean recommending another company's product if the salesman truly feels that product would better meet the needs of this customer. I'm sure this will all sound ridiculously idealistic to some salesmen, advertising executives, and executive suite top dogs. The fact is, however, that there are companies who are succeeding on the basis of this very philosophy.

None of us wants to be treated like a child so stupid he cannot see the transparency of high-pressure retailing practices. Although we may continue to buy the products, most of us are moved to scoff at the techniques, for instance, by which cigarettes are sold by associating smoking with sexual charm or masculinity. I actually marvel at the way in which soap manufacturers have convinced us that we smell so badly! Keeping in sight of our concern with manipulations, note how even guilt is used as a motivating technique in merchandising: selling insurance by making the customer feel guilty unless he provides well for his

193

children; selling tires by making the customer feel guilty unless he provides for the safety of his family; selling photographs by making the customer feel guilty unless he provides each child with a memory photograph album. I am not passing moral judgment on this since I am not sure I know what the alternatives are—in the business ethics of my own profession, I am not permitted to advertise—but I'm sure we all recognize what seedbeds exist in this environment for manipulation.

Businessmen patients and friends constantly raise the fundamental issue of how to succeed in business without really manipulating. As yet, I confess, I haven't been able to answer them very well. Is it possible that there can be a "good manipulation" in business, where a supposedly more mature person chooses for, and controls the decision of, the more immature? Can a "Thou" (spelled with a capital "T") ever decide for a "thou" (spelled with a small "t") without making him an "it" or a "thing"? Certainly such a decision would not be actualizing because the theory of actualizing is to help the more immature individual become more mature. This he cannot do if he is kept in a state of stupidity and dependence.

I realize that this all gets pretty close to the heart of our capitalistic system—it would seem to indicate that this aspect of the system needs a thorough reexamination—but, before someone accuses me of being against our free enterprise system, which I am not, let me quote the late Adlai Stevenson: "The real patriots are those who love America as she is, but who want the beloved to be more lovable. This is not treachery. This, as every parent, every teacher, every friend must know, is the truest and noblest affection." [2] I love America above all other countries and ways of life. Nevertheless, I am concerned with how can we do

194

business and yet return to our original concepts of the worth and dignity of man.

Clergymen of all faiths have wrestled with the problem for years. Businessmen are not ipso facto soulless individuals; without their sincere and open-handed support, we could not have the magnificent church structure that is a part of our way of life. Still there is the conflict, which the great psychoanalyst, Karen Horney, has posed very clearly. The contradiction, she says, is one of valuing the concept of competition in the American way of life on the one hand, and of brotherly love and humility on the other. On the one hand, we are supposed to be assertive and aggressive and push all competitors out of the way. On the other hand, clergymen tell us not to be selfish, that we should be humble, turn the other cheek, and love our neighbor rather than compete with him. The modern manipulator feels this contradiction deeply.

Psychologists and psychiatrists are called upon daily to help unravel the tangled patterns manipulating businessmen weave into their lives. The goal of our therapy is to help them find their own creative syntheses of the polarities that they all possess. As I have stated often in this book, the ultimate objective is to become the many-splendored person of complimentary opposites—the person who has found his creative synthesis. As an answer to Karen Horney's dilemma, I would suggest that the aggressive manipulator, as well as the over-sympathetic lover, can find an actualizing, creative synthesis when he becomes "assertively caring." This, of course, requires a process of therapy and is not done simply by willing it.

While the overall question remains unanswered, and I confess my inadequacy to come up with a satisfactory answer as yet, my telephone continues to ring. My therapy

195

room continues to fill up with troubled persons. For those whose manipulative habits in business have brought them to my door, I can at least offer Kant's extraordinarily creative suggestion: Be yourself; find your creative ethic within (as this book has been proposing). However, let it be possible that your inner ethic is capable of serving as a norm for mankind as a whole! To the individual businessman who has gotten into difficulty through manipulations and whose health and survival seem to demand it, I recommend that he consider the actualizing alternative, even though it may mean he will be less successful in the marketplace. As we read in Matthew 16:26, *For what is a man profited, if he shall gain the whole world, and lose his own soul?*

NOTE

1. See Abraham H. Maslow, *Eupsychian Management* (Homewood, Ill.: Richard D. Irwin, 1965).

2. P. Steiner, *The Stevenson Wit and Wisdom* (New York: Pyramid Books, 1965), p. 130.

PART IV
The Process of Actualization

CHAPTER 15
Actualization Therapy

Okay. If I am a manipulator, how then do I change into an actualizor? Or change that manipulative husband of mine —or wife, son, daughter, boss, in-law? I hope that many mild manipulators can be helped simply by reading and discussing this book with friends or discussion groups. For the more manipulative and for those seeking to understand how to become more actualizing, I offer this description of how therapeutic approaches work.

199

Actualization Therapy

Therapy is the only *systematic approach* I know of for changing manipulators into actualizors or for helping actualizing people to become more so. By "actualization therapy," of course, I refer both to the formal types of individual therapy and the various forms of group therapy or group dynamics which change manipulative trends into actualizing trends. Actualization therapy is not a new school of therapy but an emphasis on reducing manipulation and fostering actualization which a therapist of any "school" of thought may wish to emphasize.

We have found group dynamics techniques helpful in Parent Actualization Training at our Institute. This is a semi-therapeutic class for parents who meet once a week, wherein we use group discussion, role-playing, testing, demonstrations, lectures, analysis of tape recordings, and case analysis. In these groups parents learn skills and methods to help prevent their children from developing emotional problems that would require more intensive treatment. The parents also help themselves to develop into more fully functioning people.

A second example of actualization therapy is Sensitivity Training, in which we train groups of professional people in the general area of interpersonal sensitivity. The small Sensitivity Training group encourages a high level of individual participation and involvement. For instance, here is a quote from the UCLA Sensitivity Training brochure:

The small Sensitivity Training group provides an opportunity to experience yourself more fully in your relations with others—to discover at a deeper, more intensive level, what you and others are thinking and feeling, to learn how people relate to each other and how you in turn relate to them. As you come to see yourself more realistically—in terms of your values and goals, your habits and manners, your personal strengths and weaknesses, your potentials and limits—you may get a more accurate image of yourself as an instrument in interpersonal relations. Thus, you may be free yourself to function more effectively in those relations, without being excessively burdened by unrealistic assumptions about your personal adequacy, your worth, or your social acceptability.

Sensitivity Training is designed to increase social sensitivity (the ability to sense what others think and feel) and behavioral flexibility (the ability to behave appropriately in a variety of interpersonal situations).

The small Sensitivity Training groups encourage a high level of individual participation and involvement. Here, as a participant, you may expect to learn more about yourself and your impact on others; understand your own feelings and how they affect your behavior toward others; become more sensitive to the ways people communicate with each other; learn "active listening"—for meanings and for feelings; learn how people affect groups and groups affect people; learn how to help groups function more effectively.

Another very exciting technique of recent origin is "Marathon Therapy," in which a group of a dozen or so people meet for twenty-four to thirty hours of unbroken, concentrated discussion. Privacy, except for going to the bathroom, is not allowed. Meals are eaten in the therapy room. Here we have men and women thrown together for a day and night in one room and forced ultimately to be themselves. We practice total honesty, and all feelings, no matter how ridiculous, must be expressed. As the hours pass, feelings become much more transparent. Real expression—growth—results. I commend this remarkable experience to those who would truly know themselves.

Therapy, incidentally, can mean many things to many people. The degree of it necessary for any individual will depend on his needs, in the same way that he might take his car to the garage for a tuneup or major overhaul. Carl Rogers says this can be seen in eight stages, as a rising curve from zero, the worst manipulative patient, to seven, the self-actualizing person. A patient might come in, then, at stage two and wish to go to stage four; another at stage three to go to six. Each graduates from therapy at the point at which he is functioning sufficiently and efficiently for his own needs. In group therapy, on the other hand, the patient doesn't graduate until the therapist *and* group agree that he can now handle life.

It should be stressed also that not everybody needs therapy. As a matter of fact, all an individual often needs is some tender loving care. Moreover, in life there are many therapeutic experiences that help a person: good friends, a great teacher, a crisis such as a death in the family—any of these may cause significant change.

In the area of individual therapy there are various schools of thought, naturally, and no one system has proved to be the only or best way. In this chapter I will describe dimensions of therapy that are used by all therapists to a greater or lesser degree. Each should illustrate how professional psychotherapy is developing a science for creating change in people. The discussion should also be helpful to the reader as a guide to areas that need investigation and change in order to permit growth from manipulation to actualization. With each of these techniques I will define what is meant by the dimension and the theories of important psychologists who have developed it. Finally, I will suggest its application to manipulation and actualization and give some examples of these dimensions as they are used in psychotherapy.

Here, then, are the unique emphases of ten recognized approaches to psychotherapy with a discussion of their relevance to growth toward actualization.

1. *Caring.* This is the therapist's attitude of loving regard for the individual, whether expressed by unconditional warmth or aggressive, critical caring. Caring is a primary means of combatting manipulations. Erich Fromm stresses the importance of loving as a factor in the development and health of the individual in his definition of love as "the active concern for the life and growth of that which we love."

Manipulators, it will be recalled, are of two fundamental types, passive and active. Passive manipulators are helpless, indecisive, and clinging; the kind of love these people need is aggressive, critical caring. The active manipulator, on the other hand, who pouts, makes demands, and expects much from others, may need aggressive, critical caring to point out what it is he is doing. He may also need the unconditional warmth type of loving to show him that he is loved in spite of his manipulations. Finally, each may need the analytical form of loving in order to show him vividly the manipulations he is exemplifying.

Some statements the therapist might use are: I have warm feelings toward you; I think you're a louse, but I still like you; What happens to you matters to me.

2. *Ego-strengthening.* This is the therapist's development of thinking, feeling, and perceptive ability in the patient to help him cope more effectively with life.

The work of the ego-analysts, such as Ernst Kris, Heinz Hartmann, and David Rappaport, emphasizes the importance in experiencing involuntary delay, developing thinking, anticipating future events, and developing self-direction. These men underscore that man is more a pilot of his behavior and less a robot than Freud implied with his accent on unconscious and instinctual drives.

Some examples of interactions of patient and therapist to illustrate the use of ego-strengthening would be:

Patient: I love my husband.
Therapist: Would you say that again.
Patient: I love my husband!
Therapist: You sounded like you meant it that time.

Therapist: That sounds strong. You sound very strong today.

Patient: I'm beginning to see that my wife is using me.
Therapist: You really are seeing her more clearly now.

3. *Encountering.* This is the active encounter between patient and therapist, each of whom is *being* and *expressing* his real feelings. Encountering is another word for contact, which has been discussed in Chapter 5 as the substitute for control, the chief weapon of the manipulator.

The work of existentialists, especially as reviewed by Rollo May, stresses encounter as the dimension which encourages growth in the individual.[1] Thus, this newer emphasis in therapy encourages expression by the *therapist* as well as the patient as a means by which growth is fostered in the interview.

The following are examples of encountering taken from an interview between patient and therapist:

Patient: (Talks incessantly.)
Therapist: Shut up and let me talk!

Patient: (Talks in strained voice.)
Therapist: Stop the whining!

Patient: I thought my mother was acting very sweetly then.
Therapist: It seems to me your mother was acting like a bitch!

Patient: I hope you will be nice to me today.
Therapist: You are doing to me now what you do to your family. You are trying to seduce me.

4. *Feeling.* This is the provision by the therapist for experiencing a psychologically safe relationship of feelings which the individual has heretofore found too threatening to experience freely. Feeling is a very important dimension of life in which the manipulator is crippled. The psychotherapist, therefore, provides and stresses learning how to *feel* one's feelings deeply.

The work of Carl Rogers is most expressive of this dimension. He has stressed the creation of a psychologically safe relationship by attitudes of acceptance and permissiveness.[2]

Some examples of how the expression of feelings is fostered in a therapeutic relationship:

The therapist hands the patient the Kleenex box (indicating acceptance that the patient is about to cry).

Patient:	Damn it! Nothing is going right today.
Therapist:	You are feeling very angry today (showing acceptance of the feeling) .
Patient:	Boy, she really teed me off.
Therapist:	You were upset when she said those things.
Patient:	But when she invited me over for dinner, I changed my mind.
Therapist:	I gather that you felt very warmly toward her when she did that.
Patient:	(Sits silently, showing moisture in eyes, but does not talk.)
Therapist:	It hurts so much, it's hard to talk about it.

5. *Interpersonal analysis.* This is the analyzing by the therapist of the patient's perceptions or manipulations of the therapeutic relationships in life. Interpersonal analysis is a technique for analyzing the games that manipulative people play on each other.

The work of Harry Stack Sullivan stresses the concept of interpersonal relationships as a primary area of therapeutic work.[3]

Recent interpersonal analytic emphasis is found in the work of Berne and Perls[4] who stress that therapy is helping the patient understand how he misconstrues and manipulates the therapist in many ways. For example, the passive patient may play "helpless" and refuse to think for himself, trying to get the therapist to "mother" him. Or the active manipulator may have an "authority" problem and so tries to push the therapist around. It is assumed that whatever games the patient exhibits in therapy he also utilizes in his other interpersonal contact relationships in life.

Here are examples of how the manipulator is described to himself by the therapist:

Patient: (Sits and says nothing.)
Therapist: You simply sit and expect me to do the work.

Patient: (Talks of telephone call to therapist late last night.)
Therapist: You called the answering service at 3 AM this morning to punish me for supporting your husband. You just wanted to wake me up.

Patient: You just sit. You don't earn your money because you don't tell me what to do.
Therapist: You try to dominate me just like you do your children.

6. *Pattern analysis.* The therapist analyzes the patient's unworkable patterns of functioning and assists him in developing adaptive patterns of functioning.

It would seem that most people pick up a philosophy of life in a kind of smorgasbord style, without much consistency or logic. Psychotherapy helps check these ideas and provides a well-integrated frame of reference or system of meaning.

Leary's system, which underlies Figure 1 in this book, is an example of pattern analysis of personality through the bipolar expression of the love-hostility and power-weakness dimensions of personality.[5]

Frankl, in his system of therapy called "logotherapy," looks for the patterns which give the patient meaning: "The striving to find a *meaning* in one's life is a primary motivational force in man." [6]

Some examples of how the therapist gives patterns of meaning or integration to the many comments made by the patient in therapy:

Patient:	(Talks at length of how it is stupid for her to be doing things for people all the time.)
Therapist:	What's *stupid* about that?
Patient:	Well, I guess I don't know for sure.
Therapist:	Maybe it is *self-defeating* rather than stupid.

Patient:	I wasn't so hurt the last time she made that nasty comment to me.
Therapist:	You are beginning to reduce your *over-sensitivity* to others.

Patient:	I don't seem always to be so confused when I talk now.
Therapist:	You seem to be making better *sense* today. Maybe you're *not afraid* to make sense now?

7. *Reinforcing.* The therapist rewards behaviors which are growth-enhancing as well as socially adaptive and punishes behaviors which are negative or self-defeating. This learning emphasis is represented by Wolpe and Ellis.[7] They believe that man's problems are his fears and thoughts and that neurotic fears and ideas are like bad habits which have to be gotten rid of and replaced by healthy responses.

Examples of how reinforcement is used to help the patient:

Patient: (Talks about many people.)

Therapist: (When patient speaks of his mother, therapist writes notes about the comments, indicating to the patient therapist considers these comments more significant than others.)

Patient: (Talks about preparing breakfast for her husband now when she didn't used to.)

Therapist: You are finding that making your husband breakfast makes him happy. (To reinforce value of pleasing her husband.)

Patient: I didn't lose my temper for the first time in a long time.

Therapist: Didn't you get satisfaction from controlling yourself then? (To indicate the reward one obtains from control.)

Patient: (Talks of insignificant things.)

Therapist: (Remains silent, giving a negative-reinforcement. Shows the patient that this material is unimportant.)

8. *Self-Disclosing.* The exposing by the therapist of his own defensive patterns of living encourages the patient to do the same thing.

Sidney Jourard has stressed that self-disclosure is a factor in the process of effective counseling or psychotherapy. "Would it be too arbitrary an assumption," he asks, "to propose that people become clients because they have not disclosed themselves in some optimum degree to the people in their life?" [8] For instance,

Patient: Have you ever been as scared as I am?
Therapist: Scared to death.

Patient: You have never felt like that because you're a psychologist.
Therapist: The therapist is a model of a human being too, not a model of perfection. I've felt that way.

Patient: I feel ugly.
Therapist: I felt awfully ugly when I was an adolescent.

Patient: I bet you never felt lonely.
Therapist: I'm often lonely.

9. *Value reorienting.* This is the reevaluation by the therapist of the patient's loosely formulated value orientations (assumptions about self and others, and so forth) which enables the patient to commit himself to examined and operational values.

Dr. Victor Victoroff has written:

As a psychiatrist, I examine assumptions. The business of psychiatry is to inventory assumptions and to run a trace to their source in personal history. Define assumptions as ideas or principles which are held to be self-evidently, axiomatically true. They are requisite to orientations as to time, place and circumstance. They may be accepted as the result of expediency or accident or because of slavish identification with others who are admired or hated. Or they may be indictive summations, acknowledged springboards into the unknown, accepted on a frankly tentative basis until something better comes along.[9]

Victoroff's emphasis on reorientation of value assumptions is a significant part of the psychotherapeutic process. Charlotte Buhler also suggests value orientation as a chief feature of the psychotherapeutic process.[10]

For example, the following are ways a patient reorients his values and has them reinforced by the therapist:

Patient: I don't ever like to stick my neck out and let people know what I feel.

Therapist: I think it is very important that you do stick your neck out and that people do know what you feel.

Patient: Gee, I never realized how much fun it is just to live in the here and now instead of always planning for the future.

Therapist: I see you are recognizing how important it is to live in the present.

Patient: I am beginning to realize that it is important for me to say what I want and ask for it.

Therapist: I like you when you care for your own needs.

Patient: Gee, it really isn't so bad to say what I think even when I am angry.

Therapist: I think it is great when you can be assertively aggressive.

Patient: I am finding that it really is fun to be close to people.

Therapist: You really are beginning to show warmth, and I can feel it even in our relationship.

10. *Reexperiencing.* This is the reexperiencing of past influential learnings and the desensitizing of pathological effects of these learnings on one's present functioning.

Historically, psychoanalysis is a system of psychotherapy which has emphasized understanding the past as a necessity for understanding the present. Fenichel, for instance, believes that "analysis should show the past to be effective in the present." [11] For instance,

Patient: (Talks of his adolescence when he was angry at his mother.)

Therapist: Just because you were angry at your mother as an adolescent doesn't mean that you have to stay angry at her *now*.

Patient: I used to feel very close to my father when I was a small boy.

Therapist: Do you ever feel that way *here and now* with me?

Patient: (Talks of an unhappy experience with his mother and how he felt disappointed in her.)

Therapist: Make believe you can talk to your mother
              right now. Talk to her as if she were sitting
              on the couch over there.

Changing Manipulators to Actualizors
in Group Therapy

It is possible in therapeutic groups to turn manipulators
into actualizors, and the procedure, needless to say, is as
fascinating as brain surgery. The results are as gratifying
to the therapist as to the individuals involved, for there is
always a challenge when people confront one another.
Let us look in on such a session and see what happens.

They begin assembling at 7 PM in the Institute waiting
room that is warmly decorated in the atmosphere of a comfortable living room. Tonight there are eight of them, four
men and four women, since we try to balance the sexes
evenly. There is an engineer, a doctor of medicine, a
furniture salesman, a male schoolteacher, a nurse, a housewife, a woman teacher, and a pretty young secretary. Their
ages range from twenty for the secretary to fifty for the
doctor and engineer, and together they represent various
degrees of manipulating and actualizing.

All have been having interpersonal and intrapersonal
troubles. The nurse, for instance, is losing her husband
and can't understand why he doesn't think she is feminine;
the truth is she wears mannish clothes and appears rather
masculine. The housewife beside her on the circular
couch is bored; her children are raised, and she doesn't
know whether to get a job or a divorce, or both. The
woman schoolteacher would like to marry but has never
found the man. The pretty young secretary is concerned

213

because her boss is trying to seduce her—her bosses usually do and usually succeed—and she can only lament: *It's happening to me!*

The men taking their places on the couch and chairs represent a further sampling of rather common problems. The doctor has been having troubles with his wife; the handsome salesman is twice divorced and going down for a third time. The engineer, a competent technician, can't get along with people, particularly the crew of women he supervises at an aircraft plant. The male teacher wants desperately to become a school principal but never quite succeeds.

For the first third of the three-hour session I and my co-therapist will be working with them. She is an attractive, well-dressed social worker of thirty-eight, who is married, has children, and actualizes at least a part of the time. (I do not use "well-adjusted" to describe her since that would mean only that she is "adjusting" or fitting into her environment; an actualizor, on the other hand, is not a fitter but tends to resist enculturization.) Each of us has his own patients in the group, but both of us will deal with any or all of these people, depending on our spontaneous reaction of the moment.

"Well," I say to open it, "what's on your mind to night?"

It is the doctor who speaks first, an average sort of man in appearance, perhaps getting a mite plump in middle age. His eyes, I note, are slightly moist as he addresses the furniture salesman. "You really upset me last week when you told me I let myself be hurt by my wife."

This is, of course, a bit of actualizing behavior, communicating to the group some part of himself. When he is actualizing, a person quite willingly expresses feelings of sensitivity or hurt. It is passive behavior, but healthy.

The engineer bites his lip when he hears it and squirms in his chair, legs crossed and the free foot kicking. A brusque man, unresponsive with females, he doggedly plays the role of a man's man as he sees it—a real slide-rule expert who is afraid of his own feelings. Being a manipulator whose primary behavior is fixated at an active and dominating extreme, he is very uncomfortable at the moment. The doctor's frank declaration has set his right foot kicking angrily.

A psychological crisis has developed. Either he must criticize the doctor or see that the doctor's hurt has value. "Who do you want to kick?" I ask suddenly.

"I want to kick Ted," he replies, glaring at the doctor. "Women always try to make men feel guilty. The worst thing you can do is let them know you are hurt by it."

"So what's wrong with being hurt and letting people know it?" I ask.

For a half-hour we discuss this. The engineer, who has had troubles both with his mother and wife and therefore has a rejecting attitude toward women generally, is afraid of cracking up. He doesn't understand that in reality people don't crack. They melt. The body's natural way of melting is through tears. Tears are as vital a part of therapeutic growth as bleeding is of surgery. When you are cut, you bleed; when you are hurt, you cry, and all manipulators hurt inside from their internal conflicts. But the Dictators and Bullies and Judges refuse to wince and fight their tears with hostility. That is why we often get sudden bursts of anger.

"Tears," he argues, "are for women and babies. Not for men." His voice betrays anger.

"Say that again," I demand.

"Tears are not for men."

"Louder!"

"TEARS ARE . . . NOT FOR MEN!"

He is trembling. "You're shaking," I tell him. "Shake more."

He tries. His chin quivers. His eyes begin to moisten.

"*Be* your eyes!" I command.

"We feel like crying," he acknowledges and suddenly breaks into tears. "Women really hurt you!" he shouts. "I have been hurt by them all my life——."

The scene is over. The crisis is passed. He is experiencing what he has been resisting.

This man has been coming for six months to reach this point and should continue for another six. If he doesn't get scared or stop prematurely, the continuing relationship with the group may enable him to accept hurtful behavior as natural. Gradually he will incorporate hurt in his system of reacting, thereby reducing the strength of his active (so-called) "masculine" responses and increasing the strength of his (so-called) "feminine" hurt responses. If he doesn't stop therapy too soon, he will, in fact, be actualizing, and industry will have back not only a good technician but a real human being.

The therapist's behavior in such a group reflects his openness to his own active and passive potentials. He must not only passively *accept* the manipulator as a person but must also actively *frustrate* him in his areas of fixation. He frustrates attempts to resist experiencing internal conflict and the manipulator's refusal to allow his bipolarities to come into awareness. The therapist does this primarily by *describing* what he sees as the manipulator reacts in his psychological crisis. ("Who do you want to kick?" "You are shaking," and so forth.)

He focuses on the manipulator's anxiety in his polar

area of needed growth and may comment, as I did to the engineer, "What does hurting cause you to feel? What does it make you want to tell? What is your objection to feeling hurt?" The manipulator's answer is likely to be, as was our man's, "A man shouldn't show hurt like that." Then the therapist responds: "What's wrong with it?" Here, of course, the manipulator is in a double bind. He is damned if he persists in his assumption that weakness is not a healthy part of a man's expressive nature, or he must admit hurting is appropriate and change himself. The embarrassment that follows enables his equilibrium to be upset and reorganized.

Although we may deal with one or two people intensely, each person present gets involved with the dialogue between the patient and therapist who are working. Although each of us is unique and different, we are all human beings and very much the same. Identification with another human being in therapy comes easily.

The Actualized Meaning of Conflict

The meaning of "conflict" for our purposes needs further attention. In the usual interpersonal context, it means negative tensions between two people, and socially this is regarded as bad since it causes suffering and destruction. What needs to be made clear is that for the actualizor *conflict is not bad*. Indeed, there can be *creative* conflict. In the group therapy just described, for example, if the engineer had not fought the doctor's hurt feelings he never would have been able to discover his own hurting, its potential and its value.

The actualizing person welcomes criticism because he knows he can learn from it. By contesting with those who disagree with him, he learns; he reveals himself in the counterpunching and discovers his own areas of weakness. The actualizor doesn't need compliments to be happy, accepting that many we receive in the course of a day are but manipulations. "You're so wonderful, doctor!" (A constant seduction.) However, if someone he admires, and who usually is not complimentary, offers one, then the actualizor listens. When we are actualizing, we learn to appreciate differences because it is out of differences that we grow.

Most interpersonal relationships are games of domination or control, in which for the manipulator the need to win is paramount. The actualizor's alternative may be described as "creative excitement." He sees conflict as something exciting from which, win or lose, he can grow. He doesn't permit himself to become *attached* to what he might win or lose, for he knows that he is *changing,* and he identifies instead with what he can *become* from the creative conflict. Involved in this, naturally, is *faith:* faith that both parties will prove adequate to the resolution of the conflict.

Thus, in actualizing groups, conflict between individuals is a most fruitful source of growth. As the individual experiences in other group members the undeveloped facets of himself, he comes to find himself changing his patterns of equilibrium. A more healthy balance is developed between his active and passive potentials.

The Process of Actualization Therapy

The process of actualization therapy can be thought of as a progression in awareness. It falls into three fundamental stages:

1. *Description of primary manipulation.* As the patient

talks, the therapist begins to see a pattern emerging in which the individual is utilizing one or two of the basic manipulative patterns in his verbalizations. For example, he may continuously resort to the patterns of helplessness and stupidity, characteristic of the Weakling, or he may more often than not utilize the power plays and the black-mailing techniques of the Bully. Once the pattern becomes clear, the psychologist describes to the patient what seems to be his primary manipulative game or games.

Manipulations are then analyzed from the standpoint of "gains." The active manipulations are seen to have *coercive* controlling value, and the passive manipulations are seen to have *seductive* values. Gains are analyzed from the short-range as well as from the long-range viewpoint. The patient is asked to state the gains that he is receiving from the particular manipulation from the short-range point of view. For example, manipulations are most often used for the control of others, for exploiting others, for avoiding situations, for structuring time, seducing others to work for one, etc. From the long-range point of view, however, they can be shown always to be self-defeating since they alienate the individual from others and keep him immature and dependent rather than mature and self-supporting.

2. *Restoring the inner balance.* Once the basic manipulative pattern has been established, the therapist then asks the individual to exaggerate the manipulative tendency so that he might experience its foolishness when expressed to such an extreme. For example, we ask the Bully to exaggerate his hostility so that he might see himself more clearly when he is playing this game to its fullest. Secondly, we ask the patient to express the *opposite* polarities of the

manipulative pattern he is demonstrating. For example, we may ask the Weakling to try to be the Dictator to see what happens. The reason for this technique is the fundamental hypothesis that the exaggerated expression of any manipulative principle is indicative of the repression of the opposite potential. For example, the Weakling in his expression of hurt usually is covering up a strong need to be the Dictator and to express the vindictiveness that the Dictator might feel. The Clinging Vine, in his expression of dependency, is really covering up a deeper need to control others and to be the Calculator. The Nice Guy, in his attempts to make us feel guilty for contesting him, is often covering up a need to be the Bully and to express his hostility. The Protector in his need to feel his responsibility for others is often covering up his need to be the Judge and to be omnipotent.

3. *Integration.* The final step is to put both active and passive polarities into a unified working whole. In order to do this, we continue to encourage the patient to express all of his active and passive potentials so that he might appreciate that actualization involves the integration of all his polarities into a unified whole. As was said in Chapter 3, the actualizor is like an ice skater who freely skates from one potential to another, employing each creatively in his movement through life.

In this connection, the patient must realize that *self-defeating* manipulations may be transformed into *self-fullfilling* actualizing behavior once he is aware of the fact that he need not reject his manipulations, but rather that the increasing awareness of one's manipulations leads naturally to actualization. Dictators can be transformed into Leaders, and Weaklings can be transformed into Empathizers, and so on.

The study of the lives of self-actualizing persons assists at this point to understand how this transformation can take place. The interaction in group therapy with self-*actualizing* persons reinforces belief in the process. It is this understanding which creates the faith in oneself which leads ultimately to actualization.

NOTES

1. Rollo May, *Existence* (New York: Basic Books, 1958).

2. Carl R. Rogers, *Client-Centered Therapy* (Boston: Houghton-Mifflin Company, 1959).

3. Harry S. Sullivan, *The Interpersonal Theory of Psychiatry* (New York: W. W. Norton & Company, 1953).

4. Eric Berne, *Transactional Analysis in Psychotherapy* (New York: Grove Press, 1961) and Frederick Perls, *Gestalt Therapy* (New York: Julian Press, 1951).

5. Timothy Leary, *Interpersonal Diagnosis of Personality* (New York: The Ronald Press Company, 1957).

6. Viktor E. Frankl, *Man's Search for Meaning* (New York: Beacon Press, 1963), p. 171.

7. Joseph Wolpe, *Psychotherapy by Reciprocal Inhibition* (Stanford: Stanford University Press, 1958) and Albert Ellis, *Reason and Emotion in Psychotherapy* (New York: Lyle Stuart, 1962).

8. Sidney M. Jourard, *The Transparent Self* (Princeton, N. J.: D. Van Nostrand Co., 1964), p. 21.

9. Victor Victoroff, "The Assumptions We Live By," *Etc.*, XVI (1958), 17-18.

10. Charlotte Buhler, *Values in Psychotherapy* (New York: Free Press, 1962).

11. Otto Fenichel, *The Psychoanalytic Theory of Neurosis* (New York: W. W. Norton & Company, 1945).

CHAPTER 16

From Manipulation
to Actualization

As we have seen in previous chapters, the paradox is that actualization cannot be striven for, but rather that one becomes actualizing at that moment when he fully surrenders to the awareness of his own manipulations. Therefore, I conclude this book with several statements made by people in psychotherapy about their own growth from manipulation to actualization.

In these pages you meet real people, all of whom have become aware of themselves as manipulators becoming actualizors. Each has freely volunteered his story. One has been in therapy two months, another two-and-a-half years. One has been in sensitivity training only. Nevertheless, each one is an expression of awareness that has created authentic personal change.

EXAMPLE 1: Engineer, age 43.

I am a manipulator.

Two months ago I didn't know I was a manipulator. Two months ago I was the most honest, the sincerest, most unmanipulative guy I knew. I was living out a way of life of which I was totally unaware. It was a blindness which caused me to stumble and grope, causing myself and others a good deal of pain.

I came into psychotherapy with two big problems: (1) I couldn't cope with the mounting pressures of an industrial sales job, and (2) relationships with my immediate family were disturbing, and I had no relationships whatsoever with anyone outside the family. In short, my entire life was very much out of balance and not really worth living. I was scared. I felt I was drifting hopelessly toward a vast, merciless void.

In therapy I learned almost immediately that I have been basically dishonest about my feelings all my life. I expressed only the safe, positive type of thoughts and feelings, always burying the negative, dangerous, conflict-producing ones. I avoided fights and conflict by silence, inaction, indecision. This was a powerful weapon, both defensive and offensive. My wife, for example, is an aggressive fighter and contender. I was more of a passive

223

type. Therefore, it was natural (and successful) for me to contend and fight by silence, by disengagement, by utter lack of communication. It usually worked. Eventually she would get off my back. I played Weakling.

I was, I began to understand, a *passive manipulator.* I worked people; I got my way through sneaky, subtle, weak, and passive tricks.

The first awareness of these behavior patterns, which came during my third time at group therapy, fell on me heavily. I was attacked, exposed, totally undressed so that all my hidden inner weaknesses, previously secure, were revealed. It was one of the worst nights in my life.

Yet, at the same time in the very same evening, I was flooded with light and new awareness of myself. (But how it hurt!) It took me a week to recover, a week in which I thoroughly cussed my psychologist-therapist for what he had done or caused to be done. Then the new life slowly began to grow. With no small amount of fear, I began to experiment both at home and at work with new tools of *real honesty.*

One day, in the middle of a major battle with my wife, I told her things I had kept inside myself for many long years. I knew I was taking a terrible risk; yet, it felt good and right as I was saying these things for the first time. When I had gotten them all out, she said, "Don't you think I didn't know those things already. By your actions, your innuendos, your silence?" I was amazed! Being totally honest with her did not destroy her or me; in fact, it brought us closer than we had ever been. Our communications since have been growing. My honesty paid off. For the first time I broke my pattern of passive tactics, and the results were amazing.

I tried it on the job. At first it was especially scary because I was risking, I thought, my entire economic security. But try it I did. I started by telling my boss in short simple terms that a recent organizational change was increasing my workload beyond reason and that I couldn't operate under the situation. Two weeks later it changed significantly for the better. I also began to say "No" at work to people asking me to do things which I didn't have to, or shouldn't have to do. I placed a large knife on my work desk, as a symbol of cutting out unnecessary trivia.

In a very short span of time my entire work situation changed drastically. Now I am not overburdened or overpressured. I have time to plan and even create on the job. I now know and have experienced deeply the fact that all my job pressures were truly *self-induced.* I was the cause of my own (job) pressures through, basically, a lack of self-confidence.

The short-term payoff has allowed for more time for planning and creating, better relationships with co-workers and customers, better attitudes toward the job, and, perhaps coincidentally, amazing successes in new sales. I expect the long-term results to be even better.

What is the cost of giving up dishonesty in feelings, a passive way of life, and manipulation? I believe it is primarily the willingness to take *risks.*

This I am learning to do. My early successes are a great encouragement. I find this new way of living exciting and stimulating. There is a fullness to it, an eager anticipation of the future. The people in my life are suddenly very real. People are now more like people than like things.

Well, I am just a beginner, and I have much to learn about myself and life. I am still a manipulator, and I now know it, but I am now risking much to change into a more real and honest person. Nevertheless, I know I have started in a new direction and that things will never again be the same.

EXAMPLE 2: Housewife, age 25.

I am a manipulator.

I learned at an early age that I could avoid the unpleasantness of direct anger or disapproval by being weak and passive. Unfortunately, I created a barrier which grew between myself and my family, friends, and husband, and which left me isolated and emotionally numb, lonely, and depressed.

To compensate for my lack of personal contact and my growing emptiness, I became a compulsive eater. As the pounds added up, I was more miserable and resentful of my position in life. To make things worse, I didn't seem able to work or be creative, or have any desire to paint. It was as if someone had shut off the emotional valve completely. When I entered therapy, I began discovering the keys to my depression in myself.

I have had a constant compulsion to visit my parents ever since I married and left home five years ago. It was the same compulsion as wanting to eat; in both instances I felt still empty after each time. It took two months in therapy before I confronted myself and became aware of my sense of family loss.

I had always believed—had been told countless times by others—that I was so lucky to have such a close family. Though I consciously agreed, I felt uneasy underneath that I was not a part of my family—that it was my father, mother, and brother who were close.

When I finally admitted my sadness and fear to myself, I was able recently to go to my parents and tell them honestly of my fear and misery and my sense of worthlessness. For the first time I genuinely felt their love and concern. In that moment the barrier I had built was not there to block them.

The barrier has disintegrated more and more as I have been able to become a real person, a feeling person. I have begun to find true acceptance of myself, as I am, which I had always longed for without manipulating situations or people. Now I no longer feel that I must see my parents often, although I enjoy them more when I do see them.

I am working on a better relationship with my husband also. I have realized how I had not only placed myself in the roles of a submissive "under dog," the Weakling, and Clinging Vine, but had assigned him the role of "top dog" —as Judge and Leader. He was the "bad guy" who didn't appreciate poor little me. I then discovered that I had not allowed him to be close to me fearing I would lose control of the situation and its predictability. Thus, although miserable, I felt myself to be "safe."

I know that I punished my husband for supposed injustice by gaining weight; it is one sure way which I knew controlled him. Now I have become more honest with myself and can increasingly express the anger and hostility which I have felt for years and dared not express before. Slowly I am being able to *be* all my feelings. I am no longer numb; I can feel the excitement of being alive.

I am feeling more like I am integrating my strength and weaknesses. No longer is my husband the top dog and I the under dog. I have turned my weakness and dependency into sensitivity and appreciation. At the same time I am being more firm and assertive with my husband and my parents. I am more of a whole person now and not just a part-person. I am becoming actualizing. But I

227

know the harder I try to keep being it, the less I feel I am; the more I slip back. So I am learning to accept my slipping. The silly thing is that when I accept the fact that I have slipped back, I move forward more easily. The more I try to hold onto my growth, the more it slips through my fingers!

EXAMPLE 3: M.D., age 43.

I am a manipulator.

Perhaps my first attempts at manipulation began as an infant. My mother has told me that as a baby I caused her concern because I looked so still and pale and she would have to put wisps of cotton to my nose to see if I still was breathing.

As a child growing up in a mission school, I was taught to be "good." To help me, I was told my father was in heaven with God watching him. I didn't dare be a "bad" boy. I later found that I was "bad" when I displeased mother and that God may or may not have agreed with her, but I played the Nice Guy game to the hilt.

In college I single-mindedly pursued a pre-med course, rejecting the ministry which was the only other suitable choice according to my mother. When World War II came, I joined an accelerated school program and went to medical school under the Navy V-12 program. The first few semesters of medical school almost crushed me, but by hanging on and studying harder I got by. Being a "good student" replaced being a good boy.

My intern year shocked me with the weight and responsibility of being an M.D. People died in spite of my care. I started to make plans for further training in a residency which would also shelter me from life on the outside. My plans fell through, and I went into general practice with a couple of older doctors. I leaned on them for tough problems. The elder doctors replaced mother.

When I was in the Navy again during the Korean War, I realized how sheltered, unassuming, and insecure I was. Training as a flight surgeon on a tour with an air group started bringing me out of my shell. At this time I married a girl who made me feel comfortable in her presence. I didn't have to be or do anything for her. I could be my own withdrawn self.

After Korea we settled in southern California with apparent superficial instant success. Nevertheless, my devotion to my practice, my wife's withdrawing and subsequent hardening to me, and my partner's marital problems brought my house of cards down on my head. I finally lashed out at my partner and departed. Eventually I took Sensitivity Training in order to understand better my patients, and here I began to see that there might be a problem in myself. I have been on the long, slow road of therapy since. For months I would come to the group and be a passive nonparticipant. Finally, the group began to ride me about being a passive Nice Guy until I got so fed up that I started becoming alive.

Through therapy and the group I now realize how passive I have been and still am, how I withdraw from contact and manipulate others into making decisions for me. I attempt to manipulate the therapists to have them do something for me. I have made best progress when the therapist or the group totally reject what I am doing. I often see myself in my patients who lean and depend on me and never take responsibility for their own health. I am seeing with disgust how my passive, powerless mode of life is not getting the end results I want. I am still

229

unable to have an open spontaneous fight with my wife; I am unable to talk freely and with feeling with my partner, I can get peeved and sulk for days for what seem trifling instances. My mind goes blank, my will powerless. But I am becoming more actualizing. I'm more aware of the game of helplessness that I play and am becoming more free of it. I'm leaning less on my M.D. degree for security and finding more security in being a person.

EXAMPLE 4: Student, age 26.

I am a manipulator.

At times I've accomplished it by playing the part of a little girl. I knew that no one would want to hurt a child and so attempted to protect and shelter myself from others and from the perils and hardships of life.

I also have manipulated people by becoming confused and not understanding a situation when it becomes a threat to myself. How can one get through to a person if she does not know what you are talking about? Also closely related to this is my becoming intellectual rather than intimate and feeling. Very often those with whom I interact have also been intellectuals and, as such, also felt more comfortable with that level of interaction. Through both the intellectualism and the lack of understanding, I effectively kept people at a distance and put a wall around myself, screening myself from being close to people and having people close to me. I was a Calculator.

This front was effective to the extent that even in a group therapy situation, the other group members were hesitant to attack me for fear of hurting me or having me leave the situation (another of my manipulative devices). I would walk out of the group when it became threatening to myself or got close to penetrating my defense mechanisms. Therefore, in order to keep me there, the others never attacked me fully, and I had them in my control. I even have used these techniques with my therapist in that I would try to manipulate him into doing the majority of the talking during the session and telling me what to do rather than my being responsible for my own decisions and actions.

I am now becoming more self-actualizing in that I am recognizing what I am doing. Again, perhaps, my intellectualism is coming out, but I feel that I must know and realize what I am doing before I can change. I am also dropping the role of a child—I ask questions and reveal myself to others more honestly and fully, not just that which will create a favorable effect to my way of thinking. I am finding that to know everything and always be right is not conducive to close relationships with others. It is difficult, but I am admitting my failures and am entering into discussions and conversations in areas in which I do not know everything, and I do not pretend that I do. Through admitting my weaknesses and shortcomings, I am better able to accept myself and the fact that I am not perfect. This, in turn, gives me a truer picture of who I am and allows me to use fully those talents which I do possess. By accepting my fear I am on the way to overcoming it and coping with it in a constructive and healthy fashion.

I am also becoming more actualizing in that I will ask people questions which involve my relationship with them rather than remaining quiet for fear of having my feelings hurt. I also tell people what I think and feel rather than coloring it with what "should" be said or "what is nice" even if untrue. In turn, I find that such actions on my part

231

do not have a disastrous effect on my relationships with others; in fact, it strengthens my friendships and makes them deeper and more meaningful.

I can see, now, how far I have yet to go in order to be fully functioning. But when I contrast this with how far I have progressed, I am encouraged and better able to accept the responsibility for myself. I am becoming an actualizor.

EXAMPLE 5: Minister, age 36.

I am a manipulator. It takes brutal honesty to confess this fact. Confession is normally the business of the parishioner, not the preacher. To admit weaknesses, doubts, confusions, and above all, moral failures, upsets the halos that set altogether too precariously upon ministers' heads.

Therefore, while it may be highly irregular for me to do so, I confess that I am a human being. Moreover, as a human being, one of the most persistent problems with which I have to grapple is the problem of manipulation. My relationships with people are often characterized by deception, unawareness, control, and cynicism. It is not always deliberate, and it certainly isn't done cunningly but unconsciously most of the time.

Manipulation came about so naturally, I suppose. Though unuttered, the word "perfection" was the keynote of what I gathered from others (ministers and laymen alike) that I was supposed to be. I prided myself into thinking I had broken out of the ministerial mold because I didn't dress the way the stereotype dressed, or drive the kind of cars they drove, or date and marry the kind of girls they so often dated and married (stereotyped preachers' wives). Yet, I hadn't broken out of the real mold—and still haven't altogether. I am still trying to fill the role of moral authority and Judge.

I've been rather *successful* at it—or at least I have thought so. The work that I have done in every parish has been judged successful by the "powers that be," and the congregations have always been highly pleased. But in much of this success I have been losing my*self*. Only during the past two or three years have I been willing to admit that the loneliness and anxiety, emptiness and despair I saw in others only mirrored that which I was experiencing in myself. It has been a gradual and agonizing admission. One who is supposed to be accomplished in the spiritual life, an authority on living, does not leave the security of that illusion too easily. A burning and undaunted dedication to my profession as a minister was a substitute for facing my own desperate personal need and dependency upon others.

My relationship to my wife was (and to a great degree still is) a manipulative one. She has seen me as a Great Dictator, rather than a haystack of weakness, and I have propagated that illusion. There were many areas of my life that she was not allowed to enter, and there were two great errors here. First, I was not willing to bare my soul to her and admit my frailty. Second, I denied her the privilege of being herself because I saw her as one whom I needed to protect. As the Protector, I made her overly dependent, and thus I controlled her. Though she has an unusual capacity for deep feelings, I'm sure I blunted her sensitivity. She, in turn, seeking to please me, has often pretended a self she never was and never could be. Working diligently to keep from hurting her, I am sure I have hurt her deeply.

The church has been an escape for me. I have tenaciously upheld moral standards at the cost of persons and in terror of admitting my own temptations and ambiguous feelings. My work has become a "god" to whom I did daily sacrifice and an escape hatch to which I could retire from my family, the world as it really is, and myself.

Coming from a poor and uneducated family and what may be termed a "culturally deprived" background, I have intensified my ambitions to achieve. A below-par education, not indicated by the two academic degrees I have since received, has driven me to *prove* myself. As a result I have been plagued by guilt for "unholy ambition." This guilt has often driven me to desperation as I sought to cross the line between a desire to really serve as a minister and the hounding ambition to professional success.

Gradually I am beginning to accept my polarities as a person. I have pride; I am humble. I am selfish; I am unselfish. I am assertive, yet dependent. I love; I hate. I admire, yet despise. I am weak; I am dominating. I trust myself, yet am overly competitive. How much guilt have I known because of some unaware source of condemnation for the ambition which I possessed! How much joy in achievement have I missed because the achievement was all mixed up in my overall program of professional success.

Yet, the game of living has become more important now. Further, being faithful to myself, seeing my need for expression, my joy in people, my dependence upon others is of primary importance. *Winning* the game sometimes dominates, and I trod roughshod over wife, children, and parishioners, but increasingly winning in the traditional professional interpretation is decreasing in importance, and being a person—as a husband and father, then as a minister—is growing in significance.

I am a riddle and a mystery—a manipulator and an actualizor. For a long time I've sought to be something else: John Q. Minister. Buber's word is now my inspiration. "In the world to come," he said, "I shall not be asked, 'Why were you not Moses?' I shall be asked, 'Why were you not Martin Buber?' " And I shall not be asked, "Why were you not John Q. Minister?" but "Why were you not ———?" This is my continuing conversion: *I am a manipulator; I am becoming an actualizor.*

EXAMPLE 6: *Myself.*

Dr. Carl Rogers has said that there is a hunger in readers to know something of the person writing to them. As he says, what is most personal is most general—the very feelings and experiences which most of us regard as most private and most personal often turn out to be the very same experiences which others have had. Sydney Jourard calls this the need for self-disclosure, and I believe that disclosing our selves is the best way to continue to grow toward self-actualization. Therefore, in this section I am going to attempt to describe something of my life history and some of my struggles on the road from manipulation toward actualization.

Early Recollections

I was brought up in the Midwest Bible belt and received much love from my parents. At the same time, however, I was sent to Sunday School at a strict fundamentalist church. There I was taught that I should not drink, dance, go to movies, and so forth. Religion, as I saw it there, was a system of "don'ts." So I began to conceive of God as a manipulator. His emphasis seemed to be on the negatives rather than the positives—that I could only be good if I was controlled by these many prohibitions. Since then, I have come to feel that such a conception of God is too small. I now have to feel that the kingdom of God is within me and that the honest expression of my deepest feelings can also be a profound spiritual expression. I believe that everyone needs a personal religion and needs to be working continuously on the meaning of life for himself. All the great religions seem to provide us with actualized persons who serve as models for being. The persons of Jesus and the Buddha are examples.

I received love from my parents, though my mother's control was more passive than active. Questions like "What time will you be home tonight?" seemed to have much more effect on me than had she demanded that I be home at a particular hour. Since my older brother was eight years older and assisted my father in his business, he was a "top dog" to me. I was always the little brother who swept my father's sign shop on Saturdays, and so I felt very much an "under dog."

My first contact with the meaning of power in human relationship came in high school when I joined the ROTC. By working hard I rose to a Cadet Captain and became very impressed with the institutional power of the military. In the military framework, I found, I could make other people do things—that which I ordered. I could push and manipulate them in the ways I wished them to go. Here for the first time in my life I was a "top dog," and I enjoyed it. Yet, one of life's big lessons for me has been that I really cannot make anybody do anything unless they wish to. I have also found that an actualizing relationship, in which I regard another as a "thou" rather than a "thing," brings deeper psychic rewards than the power.

College and Military Life

My undergraduate years were spent at the University of Illinois, and there I learned the lessons of being a model student. Since I was always bright in school, I never had difficulty with grades, and I found also that my grades were enhanced if I played the good under-dog student which means being obsequious and submissive to the top-dog professor. My excellent transcript gives recognition to my success in this role. Only later have I come to regret that I was not more aggressive and expressive as a student. I might have learned a good deal more, even though my grades might not have been quite as excellent.

Pearl Harbor hit during my college years, and since I was again in ROTC, I was given an opportunity to train as an officer. I played the good under-dog officer candidate and was graduated from Officer Candidate School in Fort Benning, Georgia. Not long afterward, I found myself in combat in the Battle of the Bulge. At this point I discovered that the military system of absolute authority of officers seems to break down in combat when I was required for the fourth or fifth time to take out combat patrols which may not return. I found that asking rather than commanding payed off. This was one of the deep lessons which has influenced my humanistic orientation to living. In combat even the lowly G.I. will volunteer if he is treated like "thou" rather than a "thing."

Wounded in combat by a German machine gun, I had the unusual experience of being carried to safety by German prisoners and then nursed back to health in a captured German general hospital. One of the kindest, most empathic human beings I have ever met was a German nurse, a man of about the age of my older

237

brother, who demonstrated to me the power of caring as opposed to military force. Just a few weeks previously, I would have killed him on the field of combat! This dramatic change in my life situation made me realize how important it is to regard persons as persons rather than as cogs in a military machine. My experience with this German male nurse was a profound lesson in living for me.

Graduate School

After the war I enrolled for graduate work at Stanford University. In graduate school I first learned what it was to be *respected* by a professor rather than being treated simply as the under dog, as I had been back in the undergraduate days in Illinois. Professors Henry McDaniel and Ernest Hilgard, at Stanford, gave me a respect which seemed to facilitate my personal growth more than any other thing. During my graduate schooldays I also spent a summer at the University of Chicago under Dr. Carl Rogers and his students. He was a man whose very therapeutic system was based on respect for, and trust in, the self of another. During that summer I experienced what it meant to have a "Thou-Thou" relationship with others.

Being a Psychologist

When I was graduated from Stanford, I went to Pepperdine College for five years and taught under my old professor, Dr. E. V. Pullias, a deeply spiritual man and a very thoughtful and loving person. His method of democratic, rather than authoritarian, administration further gave me belief in the power of appreciation and respect. After my work at Pepperdine I went into the field and practice of psychology, in which I am still engaged. Perhaps the two men who have most influenced my life during these years have been Dr. Frederick Perls and Dr. Abraham Maslow. Dr. Perls was my therapist for a two-year period and helped me understand many of the patterns which I have described in this concept of manipulation. Dr. Maslow came to visit our Institute several years ago after seeing some of my work. I am impressed with the importance of the inspiration of such people as Doctors McDaniel, Hilgard, Perls, and Maslow toward stimulating in me a belief in myself.

Becoming a Person

In some ways I feel my success as a psychologist has been detrimental to my success as a person. I could have been a better parent to my children when they needed me most during their earlier years if I hadn't been so busy writing and developing my practice. Now that they are in their adolescence and are drawing away from their parents, I feel the hurt that comes from this. I hope that my increased sensitivity to them during their struggle in adolescence and during their adulthood may make up for some of my neglect during their early years. They have taught me more than anyone else how impossible it is to control another person. A parent does not own his children; he simply has them on loan for a few years. Finally, I am having trouble letting my teen-age children grow apart from me. I can tell my patients not to concern themselves about teen-agers who are rejecting them, but it is hard to handle my own.

I believe that I am a good therapist because I am sensitive to my own and other people's feelings, but this same sensitivity is a two-edged sword because I am very vulnerable to criticism and people who are hurtful. Instead of being as direct and expressive as I would like to be, I often handle them indirectly.

Thus, as I continue to look at my manipulations, I feel myself become more actualizing. But most of all, I feel fully my humanness as a human being who can make mistakes and still grow. A psychologist must never be a model of perfection but only a model of full humanness, for he, like every other person, is a decidedly imperfect person. We must accept ourselves as we are, not regret that we are not gods. The paradox is that when we do accept ourselves, we find ourselves growing and changing.

What I want to make clear is that as psychologists, we cannot allow our patients to make us into gods. When a patient makes a psychologist into a god, he is projecting his own strength and power onto him, and in doing so, he makes himself the weak underdog. Therefore, I am not the model of perfection—only the model of full humanness.

I realize that I am risking being judged adversely by some of the things I have revealed, but I know also that I must be that self which I truly am, no matter how foolish, silly, or ridiculous I am. That's me, and I've got to be patriotic to myself. For only by being myself (my manipulations and all) can the resulting awareness lead to increasing actualization.

Conclusion

This "inner journey" from manipulation to actualization is not a new one. This book only puts it into new terminology. To conclude, therefore, it seems appropriate that I quote Woodrow Wilson who wrote the following over sixty-five years ago:

"It is a very wholesome and regenerating change which a man undergoes when he "comes to himself." It is not only after periods of recklessness or infatuation, when he has played the spendthrift or the fool. . . . He comes to himself after experiences of which he alone may be aware: When he has cleared his eyes to see the world as it is, and his own true place and function in it. It is a process of disillusionment. He sees himself soberly . . . as well as what his powers are. . . . He has got rid of earlier prepossessions. . . . He has learned his own paces; has found his footing. It is a process of disillusionment, but it disheartens no soundly made man.[1]

It is my hope that the personal expressions in this chapter and the ideas in this book in general may guide you, the reader, in your personal adventure on the road to actualization.

NOTE

1. Woodrow Wilson, "When a Man Comes to Himself," *The Century*, XL (June, 1901), 268.

BIBLIOGRAPHY

Books

Barron, Frank. *Creativity and Psychological Health*. Princeton, N. J.: D. Van Nostrand Co., 1963.

Baruch, Dorothy W. *How to Live with Your Teen-Ager*. New York: McGraw-Hill Book Company, 1953.

Berne, Eric. *Games People Play*. New York: Grove Press, 1964.

———. *Transactional Analysis in Psychotherapy*. New York: Grove Press, 1961.

Brammer, Lawrence M., and E. L. Shostrom. *Therapeutic Psychology*. Englewood Cliffs, N. J.: Prentice-Hall, 1960.

243

Buber, Martin. *The Way of Man*. Chicago: Wilcox and Follett, 1951.

Bugental, J. F. T. *The Search for Authenticity*. New York: Holt, Rinehart & Winston, 1965.

Buhler, Charlotte. *Values in Psychotherapy*. New York: Free Press, 1962.

Burdick, Eugene. *The Ninth Wave*. Boston: Houghton Mifflin Company, 1956.

Burke, L. H., and E. L. Shostrom. *With This Ring*. New York: McGraw-Hill Book Company, 1958.

Cole, William G. *Sex in Christianity and Psychoanalysis*. New York: Oxford University Press, 1955.

Dollard, John, and Neal E. Miller. *Personality and Psychotherapy*. New York: McGraw-Hill Book Company, 1950.

Ellis, Albert. *Reason and Emotion in Psychotherapy*. New York: Lyle Stuart, 1962.

————. "Thoughts on Theory Versus Outcome in Psychotherapy," *Psychotherapy: Theory, Research, and Practice,* I (January, 1964), 83-87.

Emerson, James G., Jr. *Divorce, the Church, and Remarriage*. Philadelphia: The Westminster Press, 1961.

English, Horace, B. and A. C. *A Comprehensive Dictionary of Psychological and Psychoanalytical Terms*. New York: David McKay Co., 1958.

Farber, Leslie H. "Faces of Envy," *Review of Existential Psychology and Psychiatry,* I (Spring, 1961), 131-39.

Fenichel, Otto. *The Psychoanalytic Theory of Neurosis*. New York: W. W. Norton & Company, 1945.

Ford, Donald H., and Hugh B. Urban. *Systems of Psychotherapy*. New York: John Wiley & Sons, 1963.

Frankl, Viktor E. *Man's Search for Meaning*. New York: Beacon Press, 1963.

Fromm, Erich. *The Art of Loving*. Colophon ed.; New York: Harper & Row, [1956] 1962.

————. *The Heart of Man*, ed. Ruth N. Ashen. New York: Harper & Row, 1964.

————. *Psychoanalysis and Religion*. New Haven: Yale University Press, 1950.

Glasser, William. *Reality Therapy*. New York: Harper & Row, 1965.

Greenspoon, Joel. "The Reinforcing Effect of Two Spoken Sounds on the Frequency of Two Responses," *American Journal of Psychology* (1955), pp. 409-16.

Haley, Jay. *Strategies of Psychotherapy*. New York: Grune & Stratton, 1963.

Hogan, R. "Issues and Approaches in Supervision," *Psychotherapy: Theory, Research, and Practice*, I (1964), 139-41.

Horney, Karen. *Neuroses and Human Growth*. New York: W. W. Norton & Company, 1950.

————. *The Neurotic Personality of Our Time*. New York: W. W. Norton & Company, 1937.

————. *Self-Analysis*. New York: W. W. Norton & Company, 1942.

Jourard, Sidney M. *The Transparent Self*. Princeton, N. J.: D. Van Nostrand Co., 1964.

Jung, Carl G. *Modern Man in Search of a Soul*. New York: Harcourt, Brace & World, 1933.

Krasner, Leonard. "Studies of the Conditioning of Verbal Behavior," *Psychological Bulletin* (1958), pp. 148-70.

Leary, Timothy. *Interpersonal Diagnosis of Personality*. New York: The Ronald Press Company, 1957.

Maslow, Abraham H. *Eupsychian Management*. Homewood, Ill.: Richard D. Irwin and Dorsey Press, 1965.

————. *Motivation and Personality*. New York: Harper & Row, 1954.

————. "Innocent Cognition (as an aspect of B-Cognition)," *Notes on B-Psychology*. La Jolla, California: Western Behavior Sciences Institute, August 31, 1961.

————. *Toward a Psychology of Being*. Princeton, New Jersey: D. Van Nostrand Co., 1962.

May, Rollo. *Existence*. New York: Basic Books, 1958.

Perls, Frederick. *Ego, Hunger, and Aggression*. George Allen and Unwin, 1947.

Perls, F., *et al. Gestalt Therapy*. New York: Julian Press, 1951.

Riesman, David. *The Lonely Crowd*. Garden City, N. Y.: Doubleday Anchor Books, 1950.

Robinson, Marie N. *The Power of Sexual Surrender*. Garden City, N. Y.: Doubleday & Company, 1959.

Rogers, Carl R. *Client-Centered Therapy*. Boston: Houghton Mifflin Company, 1959.

————. *On Becoming a Person*. Boston: Houghton Mifflin Company, 1961.

————. "Persons or Science? A Philosophical Question," *American Psychologist*, X (1955), 267-78.

Ruch, Floyd L. *Psychology and Life*. 6TH ed.; Chicago: Scott, Foresman & Company, 1963.

Shostrom, E. L. *Caring Relationship Inventory*. San Diego: Educational and Industrial Testing Service, 1966.

————. *Personal Orientation Inventory*. San Diego: Educational and Industrial Testing Service, 1964.

Shostrom, Everett L., and L. M. Brammer. *The Dynamics of the Counseling Process*. New York: McGraw-Hill Book Company, 1952.

Skinner, B. F. *Verbal Behavior*. New York: Appleton-Century-Crofts, 1957.

Sullivan, Harry S. *The Interpersonal Theory of Psychiatry*. New York: W. W. Norton & Company, 1953.

Tillich, P. *The Courage to Be*. New Haven: Yale University Press, 1952.

Torrance, Ellis P. *Guiding Creative Talent*. Englewood Cliffs, N. J.: Prentice-Hall, 1962.

Watts, Alan W. *The Wisdom of Insecurity*. New York: Pantheon Books, 1949.

White, Robert W. *The Study of Lives*. New York: Atherton Press, 1963.

Wickes, Frances G. *The Inner World of Childhood*. Rev. ed.; New York: Meredith Press, 1966.

Bibliography

Williams, R. L., ed. *The Young Americans*. New York: Time-Life Books, 1966.

Wolpe, Joseph. *Psychotherapy by Reciprocal Inhibition*. Stanford: Stanford University Press, 1958.

For Further Help

Workshops

Individuals and groups desiring assistance in conducting workshops on actualization therapy may write to Institute of Therapeutic Psychology, 205 West Twentieth Street, Santa Ana, California 92706, for program materials. Assistance is available at two levels: (1) materials and films for lay groups; and (2) materials and training for professionals who may wish to conduct actualization groups. The staff is also available for assistance with lay groups or for conducting workshops.

Films

The author and co-therapist Nancy Ferry presented on KHJ-TV in Los Angeles a series of TV programs on actualization therapy. The series, produced by Lawrence Schwab, is now available on film for television and for professional and educational groups which may wish to understand in greater depth the principles described in this book. These films may be shown to professional and educational groups (e.g., classes in personality and mental hygiene) and could then be used as a model for group discussion on relevant issues related to achieving actualization.

The film series, "Themes from Actualization Therapy," includes seven films, as follows: (1) Risking Being Our Selves, (2) Freedom and Actualization, (3) Aggression and Actualization, (4) Manipulation and Actualization, (5) The Divorce from Parents, (6) Self-Disclosure of the Therapist, (7) From Deadness to Aliveness. Each film is 48 minutes in length—16 MM, black and white.

Another film entitled "Maslow and Self-Actualization" is

also available, in which Abraham Maslow discusses the various dimensions of self-actualization. It is illustrated by the lives of four persons deemed to be "self-actualizing." The film is one hour in length—16 MM color. For brochure write to:

Psychological Films
205 W. 20th Street
Santa Ana, Calif. 92706

INDEX

Index

Index

Index